GW01066305

Arts: A second-level course
Understanding Music: Elements, Techn

UNIT 1

INTRODUCING RHYTHM

UNIT 2

PART 1: MORE ABOUT RHYTHM
PART 2: INTRODUCING PITCH

UNIT 3

STARTING WITH STAFF NOTATION

The Open University

The Open University, Walton Hall, Milton Keynes MK7 6AA

First published 1994. Reprinted 1997, 2000

Edited, designed and typeset by the Open University.

Printed in the United Kingdom by Selwood Printing Ltd., Burgess Hill, West Sussex

This text forms part of an Open University second-level course. If you would like a copy of *Studying with the Open University*, please write to the Central Enquiry Service, PO Box 200, The Open University, Walton Hall, Milton Keynes, MK7 6YZ. If you have not already enrolled on the course and would like to buy this or other Open University material, please write to Open University Educational Enterprises Ltd, 12 Cofferidge Close, Stony Stratford, Milton Keynes MK11 1BY, United Kingdom.

ISBN 0 7492 1116 4

1.3

UNIT 1

INTRODUCING RHYTHM

Prepared for the Course Team by Richard Middleton (with material begun by Trevor Herbert in Section 4)

CONTENTS

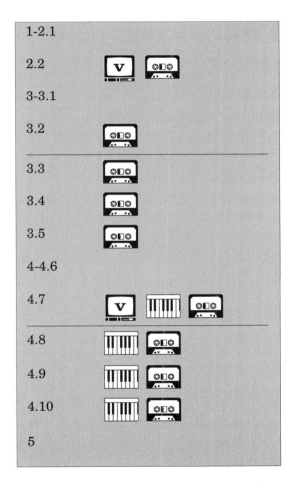

All audio items for this unit are on Audio-cassette 1.

All video items for this unit are on Video-cassette 1.

1 CONTENT AND AIMS

In the Course Introduction, you learned that music can be regarded as the product of various *elements* working together. And you got some idea of the role rhythm plays in this. Now we need to think in more detail about rhythm, an element which many people beginning to study music find confusing. There is no reason why you should be confused, provided you learn to use the basic terms with precision and to link them with the appropriate aspects of what you hear. This unit is devoted to helping you achieve that.

My aims, then, are:

1   to introduce and explain the basic terms that you will need in order to understand rhythm;

2   to help you acquire the skill of hearing rhythmic patterns, including the framework of *beat* and *metre*, with precision;

3   to introduce and explain the symbols and methods used to notate rhythms, and give you practice in using them;

4   to help you, and give you practice, in *linking* what you hear and what you see; two types of exercise will be especially helpful for this: playing notated rhythms, and writing down heard rhythms.

As well as this unit, you will need:

1   some sheets of lined paper (or plain paper on which you can rule single lines);

2   your audio-cassette player and Audio-cassette 1;

3   your video-cassette player and Video-cassette 1;

4   your keyboard (from Section 4.7 on).

This introduction to rhythm carries on into the first part of Unit 2. Although Unit 1 should comprise a reasonable week's work, it will therefore be no great problem if it spills over slightly into week two – or indeed if you finish it before the end of week one.

2 WHAT IS RHYTHM?

2.1 GENERAL CONTEXT

First, let's think a bit about rhythm in general rather than in a specifically musical context. Many of our experiences have a rhythmic quality. For example, we hope you will quickly get into a 'rhythm of study'. People speak about the 'rhythm of the seasons', and historians might refer to 'the inexorable rhythm of events'. Anyone who has milked a cow knows how irritating it is if someone bursts in and 'upsets your rhythm'. Football commentators sometimes talk of a 'rhythmic build-up of passes'. Now, what common features do these references to rhythm share? What do they tell us about the meaning of the word?

 STOP AND THINK.

My thoughts

Three aspects seem important to me:

(a) All the examples have to do with *duration* – with the passage of time.

(b) They all imply that time is *broken up, structured,* in some way: event follows event, season follows season, pass follows pass, one period of study follows another. And each event *marks its presence*; it's felt as a kind of *stress* or *accent* within the flow of time.

(c) Often there is a suggestion of *regularity,* or at least *predictability*: events succeed each other at a certain rate; they occur at (more or less) predictable moments.

Looking at it like this, you can easily see why people often regard rhythm as a basic quality of life itself. The evolution of life divides into a series of cosmological, geological and biological stages (or, as Genesis has it, into a sequence of six days' work). The rhythm of human existence is defined by birth and death. Each individual survives through physical rhythmic processes: heartbeat, breathing, eating, hormonal cycles, and so on. The organization of social life is shot through with rhythmic structures – week and weekend, annual holidays and festivities, the rota of meal-times – and our language with rhythmic allusions – 'just a minute', 'hour by hour', a 'special moment', 'heart beating faster', 'pulse racing' and so on. Music, we could say,

draws on the rhythmic quality of experience and applies this in the particular sphere of organized sound patterns. Small wonder that some anthropologists have suggested not only that rhythm is fundamental to music but also that musical rhythm, through the connection to movement, is a more fundamental distinguishing feature of human nature even than the development of language.

2.2 INTRODUCING RHYTHM

 VIDEO NOTES
UNIT 1, VIDEO SECTION 1

Introduction

This video section is about rhythm. You should watch it before reading on in the unit.

NOW WATCH THE VIDEO SECTION.

Summary

Rhythm is created by giving sounds different lengths and by giving them different amounts of stress. Real music can make great use of the simple rhythmic phenomena discussed in the video section.

Audio-cassette Item 1 is the closing moments of Stravinsky's *Symphonies of Wind Instruments*. There are comparatively few changes of pitch in this passage, or of timbre (though they are not unimportant). The most important aspect seems to be the rhythmic structure, created by (a) variations in note-length and (b) variations in stress or accent.

 LISTEN NOW TO ITEM 1 ON THE AUDIO-CASSETTE.

Figure 1   Portrait of Igor Stravinsky (1882–1971) by Pablo Picasso, May 1920 (approximately the time of the composition of the Symphonies of Wind Instruments*)*. Musée Picasso, Paris

We are now in a position to define rhythm.

> The word **rhythm** refers to music's *temporal structure* – the way its 'timescape' is organized. This structure is the product of two processes, first the manipulation of *duration* (how long sounds last) and second, the manipulation of *accent* (how much stress sounds carry).

CHECKPOINT

That definition summarizes what you have learned in this section. Make sure you understand it before proceeding.

3   THE BASIS OF RHYTHMIC STRUCTURE

3.1   INTRODUCTION

All music has rhythm; musical sounds have definite durations and definite levels of accent. But what about the other aspect in my initial formulation (Section 2.1), the element of regularity or predictability? It is this element which creates a sense of rhythmic *pattern*, and gives rise to two important rhythmic concepts: *beat* and *metre*. This section is devoted to helping you to an understanding of beat and metre. Don't worry about what these two words mean for the moment; definitions will be introduced shortly.

3.2   IS RHYTHM ALWAYS PATTERNED?

Almost all the music you will study on this course – and indeed most music anywhere – contains some form of rhythmic pattern. But some music does not. At the risk of seeming to digress, I would like to spend a few minutes discussing this basic distinction. I think it will help you to grasp the significance of rhythmic pattern if you can also identify and appreciate the effect of its absence. At the same time, if you find the non-patterned examples hard to 'understand', you shouldn't worry; as I said you won't be studying much music of that sort on this course.

Rhythmic pattern is created through some element of consistency in either durations or accents or both. That is to say, the note-lengths relate to each other in mathematically simple forms (one is the same length as another, twice as long, half as long, etc.); and accented notes occur at predictable, often regular moments. Bearing this in mind, I want you to listen to two extracts, one containing rhythmic pattern, the other not.

Exercise

Which of Items 2 and 3 on the audio-cassette is rhythmically patterned, and which isn't?

 LISTEN NOW TO ITEMS 2 AND 3.

Discussion

Item 2 seems strongly patterned to me. Most of the notes are the same length; many are quite strongly accented and these come when you expect them to.

Item 3, by contrast, creates little or no sense of pattern. Note-lengths are fantastically varied and apparently arbitrary; accenting seems to be unpredictable. The music sounds improvisatory, unplanned. (You might justifiably have pointed out that this piece does fall clearly into *short sections,* and these do follow a recurring pattern, a pattern defined mostly by the descending shape of the melody. Although musical analysts do sometimes talk of sectional patterns as having a rhythm, I shall restrict the term 'rhythm' to the note-after-note level of organization.)

I hope your response to that exercise was similar to mine. As a check, try the same exercise with two different pieces, which appear as Items 4 and 5.

Exercise

In Items 4 and 5, which is rhythmically patterned and which isn't.

 LISTEN NOW TO ITEMS 4 AND 5.

Discussion

Item 4 is **ensemble music** (that is, music for a group of performers) not solo song, and the rhythmic combinations are much more com-

plex than in Item 2 (indeed, they are extremely subtle). Nevertheless, I get a strong sense of rhythmic pattern, with note-lengths related to each other in simple, consistent ways, flows of notes of equal lengths, and accented notes recurring at regular intervals. At first, or even second, hearing you may not fully appreciate the intricate ways in which individual sounds are fixed within the overall rhythmic tapestry (I certainly didn't). But there is clearly a repeating framework.

Item 5 is also ensemble music; but I can hear no evidence of rhythmic pattern in this music. There is certainly rhythmic *interest* – ebbs and flows of movement, spurts of notes and pauses are important – but to my ear no framework, no predictability. It is as if the composer deliberately tried to avoid all semblance of regularity (I think he probably did).

I hope you have grasped the basic distinction I am trying to make – aurally as well as conceptually. And perhaps you would agree that rhythmically unpatterned music has a character of its own and is by no means devoid of rhythmic *interest*. Sometimes composers *play* on the contrast between rhythmically patterned and unpatterned music. Item 6 exemplifies a widespread East European 'folk' tradition of beginning with a rhythmically free introduction, as if to set the scene, and then breaking into a clearly patterned style, often with a strong dance rhythm. Similar contrasts can be found in more élite traditions. For instance, a good deal of opera includes not only songs (or **arias**, to use the Italian term) but also **recitative**, a kind of speech-song style designed to carry the story; the contrast is a basic feature, as Item 7 demonstrates. In recitative, the lack of consistent rhythmic pattern results from the fact that the vocal line follows the varied syllable lengths and accentuation of the words, whereas in arias the words are fitted into the patterned rhythmic framework of the music. And indeed, you might consider the musical contrast of patterned and unpatterned rhythm as analogous to that of poetry and prose.

 LISTEN TO ITEMS 6 AND 7.

Now, back to *beat* and *metre*. And, as I said, if you had difficulties with Section 3.2, don't worry too much; the basic distinction is the important thing, and you can come back to the listening later in the week, when your confidence will be greater.

3.3 BEAT

In Items 2 and 4, and in the patterned sections of Items 6 and 7, the factor which, probably more than any other, is responsible for the rhythmic regularity is the presence of a *beat*. You may have used this word in your response to these pieces, and indeed it is usually not difficult to *feel* the beat in music. It is not quite as easy to put together a general definition. But let's try.

> **Beat** is a framework underpinning music's rhythmic activity; it comprises a sequence of regularly recurring stresses.

In more vernacular language, the beat is what your foot taps to, what the conductor *beats*; it is what the parading soldier, following the bass drum, marches to, and what *beats* into the disco dancer's brain.

Again there are links with non-musical phenomena. In many natural processes, a patterned sequence of 'marked' (accented) events produces a framework against which less marked, perhaps less predictable, activity can take place. The varied events that we experience each day occur within a structure defined by the certainty of sunrise following sunrise.

In a moment, I want you to listen to Item 8. You will hear, first, a regularly pulsing sound – a *beat*. After a while, this is joined by a flow of even, shorter notes over the top; there are two of these shorter notes to each beat, and they may help you to hear that the beat *is* regular. I want you to clap with the beat. When the beat stops temporarily, keep it going with your claps, aligning these with the shorter notes. And when both beat *and* shorter notes are suspended, you must keep the beat going on your own. Check that your claps are in the right place when the beat resumes. Do this as often as necessary until you're confident that you can both *hear* a beat and *clap* one.

 LISTEN TO ITEM 8 AND DO THE CLAPPING EXERCISE.

You will realise now, I'm sure, that, as I said earlier, the beat is a *framework*: other rhythmic patterns (in that case, the shorter notes) go on around it. Moreover, even if there is no actual sound on a beat, it still exists, in your mind, continuing to provide a structure for the rhythm.

Now let's try something similar with some real music. Items 9 and 10 are both from pieces with a clear regular beat. The first is a march, the second a dance. You should be able to hear, feel and clap the beat without too much difficulty.

 LISTEN NOW TO ITEMS 9 AND 10.

Again, make sure you can hear the beat and clap along with it.

3.4 METRE

Item 11(a) is the same as part of Item 8 except for a slight modification to the beat. Item 11(b) repeats the relevant part of Item 8 unmodified.

Exercise

Listen to Item 11(a) and then to Item 11(b). Can you pick out what the modification is?

 LISTEN NOW TO ITEMS 11(a) AND 11(b).

Discussion

In Item 11(a), each alternate beat is stressed – so overall there is a strong–weak pattern:

s   w   s   w   s   w   s   w

In other words, the beat is grouped.

In Item 11(b), though, there's no grouping. The beats are acoustically identical.

 LISTEN AGAIN TO ITEMS 11(a) AND 11(b).

Check that you can hear and feel the difference.

I wonder, though, whether you actually did hear the beat in Item 11(b) as ungrouped. Just check on this.

 LISTEN YET AGAIN TO ITEM 11(b).

Make a positive effort to hear each beat in Item 11(b) as identically stressed.

Did you find you could? I imagine you found that it was impossible to do this. Apparently, the human brain, when presented with a stream of identical events, always carries out a grouping procedure: some events (beats) are given an (artificial) stress in our mind.

Did you hear the beat in Item 11(b) in groups of two

or in groups of three?

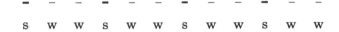

Either is possible. Try hearing it the other way from your original choice. You can do the same thing with the acoustically identical ticks of a digital clock. (Notice that we talk about the 'tick-tock' of a clock, not the 'tick-tick-tick…'; we mentally and linguistically *group* the ticks.)

The distinction between groups of two and groups of three is fundamental in almost all rhythmic processes. Basically, then, grouping beats is a question of whether stress falls on every second or third beat.

Next on the cassette, Items 9 and 10 are repeated. This time, concentrate on the grouping of the beat. In Item 9 (the march) it's grouped into twos; in Item 10 (the dance), into threes. Make sure you can hear this. Midway through each passage, I give you some help, by counting over the music.

 LISTEN TO THE REPEATS OF ITEMS 9 AND 10.

If you found this difficult, count with the beat yourself, starting on a strong beat, thus:

either

1	2	1	2	1	2	1	2	1	2	1	2
–	–	–	–	–	–	–	–	–	–	–	–
s	w	s	w	s	w	s	w	s	w	s	w

or

1	2	3	1	2	3	1	2	3	1	2	3
–	–	–	–	–	–	–	–	–	–	–	–
s	w	w	s	w	w	s	w	w	s	w	w

You should find you are forced into the right pattern. Try the *wrong* pattern – count twos to Item 10, threes to Item 9 – and it should feel obviously wrong.

The technical term for the grouping of beats is *metre*.

Metre is the grouping of beats by means of regular stress patterns.

And the term for what I have been calling a group is a *bar*.

A **bar** is a single metrical group.

In scores, as you will see shortly, bars are indicated by bar-lines – vertical lines dividing one bar from the next – something like this:

or

```
   |               |               |
 - | -   -       - | -   -       - | -   -
   |               |               |
 1   2   3   | 1   2   3   | 1   2   3   |
```

Exercise

Listen to Items 12–15 and say how many beats to the bar there are in each case. As a first step, make sure you can identify the beat, by clapping along with it. Bear in mind that it might not have the same speed in the different extracts; sometimes it might be fast, sometimes slow. When you have the beat clear, go on to the question of how many beats there are in each bar.

 LISTEN NOW TO ITEMS 12–15.

Answer

Both Items 12 and 14 have two beats to a bar. Notice that in the first the beat is quite slow while in the second it is quite fast.

Items 13 and 15 both have three beats to a bar. Again there is a disparity in speed, the first having a fast beat, the second a considerably slower one.

It is important to remember that the same metre can be found at a wide variety of different speeds.

3.5 RHYTHMIC LEVELS

Two-in-a-bar and three-in-a-bar metres are common; but so is four-in-a-bar. And this introduces a complication that we need to explore a little bit.

Four-in-a-bar is usually represented as having not two but three levels of stress:

```
 1   2   3   4  | 1   2   3   4  |
 -   -   -   -  | -   -   -   -  |
 s   w   m   w  | s   w   m   w  |
```

Beat three is of *middling* strength – stronger than two and four but weaker than one. But, sometimes it's possible to hear it in a metrically simpler way, as if it is 'in two'; in this case, beats one and three become the two beats of a two-beat bar and beats two and four become subdivisions of the beat.

```
| 1   2   3   4 |              | 1  and  2  and |
| -   -   -   - | is heard as  | -       -      |
| s   w   m   w |              | s       w      |
```

The most crucial factor in this is probably tempo.[1]

Tempo is the speed of the beat.

Item 16 starts by reproducing Item 11, which is two-in-a-bar, as you will remember. But then, as the tempo gradually slows down, the quicker notes played above the beat (that is, the subdivisions of the beat) start to sound like beats in their own right: two-in-a-bar turns into something more like four-in-a-bar.

```
| -  -  -  -  | -  -  -  - |            | -  -  -  -  | -  -  -  - |
| -     -     | -     -    | becomes    | -     -     | -     -    |
| 1     2     | 1     2    |            | 1  2  3  4  | 1  2  3  4 |
```

As the tempo increases again, four turns back into two.

---

[1] As often in musical terminology, this is an Italian word, literally meaning 'time'.

LISTEN TO ITEM 16 NOW.

As a rule it is quite obvious which unit of duration (which note-length) constitutes the beat, but occasionally there is some ambiguity. Depending on details of performance – especially tempo – and sometimes on how you choose to listen, the rhythmic structure can be heard in different ways. Thus you might hear a conductor say to an orchestra, 'this is notated in four but I want you to feel it in two'. She means that beats two and four in the four-beat grouping should become so light that they are not heard as beats in their own right but as subdivisions of two-beat groups.

Similarly, some of Beethoven's fast movements headed 'Scherzo'[2], though notated as if three-in-a-bar, are to be played so fast that they usually sound as if 'in one': and in fact, the conductor will probably beat just the first beat in each written bar, so that

becomes

1   and   and   2   and   and   1   and   and   2   and   and

Item 17 gives you a piano arrangement of the opening of the Scherzo in Beethoven's Fifth Symphony, starting off rather slowly, then repeated over and over at gradually increasing speed. At first, the music sounds as if it is definitely three-in-a-bar: the first four notes of the tune, played in Beethoven's original score by cellos and double basses, are each one beat

long. But as the tempo increases to something like normal, beats two and three turn into subdivisions, and two old bars (six beats) turn into one new bar (two beats).

 LISTEN NOW TO ITEM 17.

Go straight on then to the repeat of Item 10 following Item 17, and, as an experiment in aural imagination, try to make yourself hear it not in three but in two slow beats, with subdivisions. Count not 'one-two-three' but 'one-and-and', and beat a down-beat, as a conductor would, on each 'one'.

LISTEN TO THE REPEAT OF ITEM 10 FOLLOWING ITEM 17.

We can sum up the point of this discussion more precisely and at the same time more abstractly by means of a model of rhythmic levels; and this will also be of help to you for your work in the rest of this unit, and in the first part of Unit 2.

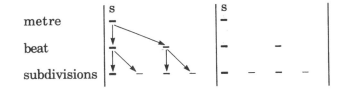

The diagram represents two bars from the beginning of Item 16. Each bar is divided into two beats; each beat is further subdivided into two shorter notes. Rhythmic structure, then, is made up of activity on three levels: metre; beat; subdivisions of the beat. The levels are related to each other in simple mathematical ways: each is formed by dividing the next higher level into groups of twos (as here) or, alternatively, threes.

Usually the levels are clear and distinct. Occasionally one level can change into a different one, probably through adjustments to tempo. In any case, the interrelationships of the three levels are crucial, not only for how rhythm is heard, but also for how it's notated – as you will see in the next section.

---

[2]   This is another term of Italian origin. Its literal meaning is 'joke'.

CHECKPOINT

You should now be able to:

1 understand the definitions of **beat**, **metre**, **bar** and **tempo** given above;

2 understand the concept of *rhythmic levels* discussed in the previous section;

3 pick out the beat in Items 2 and 8–17;

4 distinguish between two-in-a-bar and three-in-a-bar metres in Items 9–15.

If you are having difficulty with anything covered by 3 and 4 in this list, come back to it during the next couple of weeks. For hearing rhythm, little and often works best.

4 THE NOTATION OF RHYTHM

4.1 INTRODUCTION

The aim of this section is to teach you the basics of rhythm notation. This is sometimes regarded as complex but the principles are straightforward. Unfortunately, the notation we use today evolved from several different systems; as a result, rhythmic patterns can sometimes be notated in more than one way. Also there can be slight variations in the way different writers and publishers draw or print some of the symbols. Don't worry about either of these complications at the moment. I am going to guide you through the simplest route even though it means ignoring some of the subtleties.

Because we're now concerned with notating rhythm, it doesn't follow that you can stop listening. It's of no use to be able to write down the symbols if you can't also *hear* the rhythmic patterns which that notation represents. So it's vital that you conscientiously do the exercises I give you.

In Section 3.5 I introduced the idea of rhythmic levels and pointed out that each level can be regarded as dividing the level above into either two or three equal parts. Hang on to this idea. The system of rhythm notation is based on these simple arithmetical processes. It follows that rhythmic symbols don't possess absolute duration. We can't say that a particular symbol lasts for one second, or half a second (or whatever). All we can say is that one symbol is twice or half or a third as long (or whatever) as another. In other words, rhythmic values are *relative*. This is because a piece can be performed at a variety of *tempi*. Whether a church organist likes the hymns slow or fast makes absolutely no difference to the way they are notated.

4.2 THE BASIC NOTE VALUES

Here is a list of the most common rhythmic values.

⊩○⊩ = *breve*. This is the longest note value (rarely encountered today).

○ = *semibreve*, which, logically, is half the length of a breve. The semibreve is now the longest note value in common use; the American term for it is 'whole note'. Each subsequent note symbol has half the value of the preceding symbol, as follows (the American term for each is given in brackets). A semibreve is twice as long as …

♩ = *minim* (half note). This is twice as long as …

♩ = *crotchet* (quarter note). This is twice as long as …

♪ = *quaver* (eighth note). This is twice as long as …

♪ = *semiquaver* (sixteenth note).

All that information can usefully be summarized in the form of a chart.

1 semibreve

is equal in duration to

2 minims

or

4 crotchets

or

8 quavers

or

16 semiquavers

This system can in theory be extended indefinitely, with shorter and shorter notes having more and more 'tails' or 'beams'. In practice you will not often meet notes shorter than demisemiquavers (♪ or 𝅘𝅥𝅲).

Incidentally, you might wonder why the longest note value is called *breve* (i.e. brief). This is because in the Middle Ages, when it was first used, it was the shortest.

4.3 NAMING OF PARTS

You may now have some practical questions about how to write these symbols – and you may have noticed that quavers and semiquavers have already appeared in more than one form. Here are some guidelines.

1 The egg shaped, or round part of the symbol is called the *head*. Sometimes it is open:

while sometimes it is filled in:

2 All notes shorter than a semibreve have a line that runs vertically from the head; this is called the *stem*. The stem can go up from the right of the head ♩ or down from the left ₤. Whether the stem goes up or down has no effect at all on the length of the note but is entirely to do with neatness on the written page. As a general rule:

(a) Notes which have their heads *below* the middle line on the stave have the stem going up. (If you need to remind yourself about the five-line stave, look back at the Course Guide.)

(b) Notes which have their heads *above* the middle line on the stave have the stems going down.

(c) Notes which have their heads *on* the middle stave line can have their stems going either way.

3 At the end of a quaver stem is a *tail*: ♪ or ⌐. The semiquaver has two tails: ♪ or ⌐.

4 It is often the case that, instead of having tails, the stems of notes such as quavers and semiquavers are joined together by *beams*. So, for example

♪♪ may be written ♫; or ♪♪♪♪ may be written ♬; or ♪♪♪ may be written ♬. Whether or not beams are used depends entirely on whether or not their use makes the music easier to read. There are rules concerning the use of beams. It's not necessary to learn them all at this stage – you will pick them up as you go along – but the fundamental rule is that beaming should make clear the beat structure of the music. Thus, for example:

It's important that you should be able to draw all the rhythmic symbols fluently and legibly. Here are some hints. Always start with the head. Make sure it is egg-shaped: (◦). If you want a minim, add a stem, up or down: (♩). If you want a crotchet, quaver or semiquaver, fill in the head (•), then add the stem: (♩). For quavers and semiquavers, add tails or beams (♪, ♫) etc. When you come to work on five-line staves, you will need to be careful that your note-heads lie *exactly* between two stave-lines

or *exactly* on a line

But in this unit, since we're not yet concerned with notating pitch, we will make do with a single line in place of the five-live stave.

Exercise

Rule a single line on some plain paper. Practise drawing all the symbols described above. Place the note-heads on the line, and practise doing stems up and stems down. If you have never done any music writing before, this will feel strange; but you will soon get the hang of it.

4.4 RESTS

In Video Section 1 I mentioned the importance of silence in music. But if we're to have silences as well as sounds, how are we to notate them? We use *rests*. Each of the note-values you have learned has an equivalent rest, and this operates in exactly the same way rhythmically as the note; thus a crotchet rest occupies the same length of time as a crotchet note, and it is twice the length of a quaver rest, half the length of a minim rest, and so on. Here is the complete list:

⊞ = breve rest. Usually this fits between the middle line and the line above, thus:

🝙 = semibreve rest. Usually this hangs from the fourth line up of the stave, thus:

🝙 = minim rest. Usually this sits on the middle line, thus:

𝄽 = crotchet rest

𝄾 = quaver rest

𝄿 = semiquaver rest

(An alternative notation for the crotchet rest is a backward quaver rest: ɼ . This course will not use this alternative notation.)

As with the system of note-values, the system of rests is extensible. Thus a demisemiquaver rest adds a further little curl to the semiquaver rest, like this 𝄿 , and so on. Again as with note-values, there are rules governing the usage of rests: which ones to use in particular situations, in which order. But again you don't need to worry about these rules for the moment: you will pick them up in due course. (The easiest way is by looking at real scores.)

Exercise

Rule a single line and practise drawing all the rests. The only tricky one is the crotchet: it has a sort of backward s-shape

𝄽

with a curl on the bottom

𝄽

Crotchet, quaver and semiquaver rests can appear anywhere on the five-line stave, but usually they're found in the middle. With a single line, write them across the line:

4.5 TEMPO AND METRONOME MARKS

As you will remember, note symbols indicate relative values of duration. So how can we give them definite values? This, of course, has to do with tempo. At a slow tempo, a semibreve (say) will last longer than a semibreve in quicker music. One way of telling performers what the tempo of a piece should be is by using words. Often 'fast' or 'moderately fast' (or whatever) is written at the beginning of a score (or in many cases the Italian equivalent of these phrases: *allegro* or *allegro moderato*). Another, more precise, method is to give a *metronome mark*.

The **metronome** was invented in the early nineteenth century. It is a mechanical (or these days, often an electronic) device which sounds a regular click, and this is taken to represent the beat. It can be set for any tempo and, once set and started, will not vary from it. The metronome allows the composer to indicate to the performer an exact speed. This is done by a simple indication. For example, ♩ = 100 means that the tempo should be such that 100 crotchets are sounded in a minute. Similarly, ♩ = 60 means that sixty crotchets are to be counted to the minute – or one per second. In this case, the *beat* proceeds at a speed of one per second.

You will remember that usually beats are *grouped* into *bars*. (If you don't remember, look back at Section 3.4.) Most commonly (though not always) the crotchet is chosen as the note-value to represent the beat. Thus, in music which is four-in-a-bar, and which has a metronome marking of ♩ = 60, each bar, containing four crotchet beats, will last for four seconds. There will be $60 \div 4 = 15$ bars per minute.

4.6 TIME SIGNATURES

We can tell how many beats there are in a bar by *listening* to music, of course. But how do we know which note-value represents the beat in the score? To give performers this information, and to tell them the number of beats in a bar *before* they hear the music, the metre of a piece is usually indicated right at the start by means of a *time signature*.

A **time signature** looks like a fraction and is placed at the beginning of a piece of music ($\frac{4}{4}$ for example). It indicates the metre of the piece.

We will start our exercises using metres with time signatures that are easy to understand. They work as follows:

1 The upper figure indicates *the number* of beats in a bar.
2 The lower figure indicates *the type* of beats in each bar, using the following code:

8 = quaver (remember the American '*eighth* note')

4 = crotchet (or *quarter* note)

2 = minim (or *half* note)

So a time signature of $\frac{2}{4}$ (pronounced 'two-four') indicates that each bar has the equivalent of two crotchets in it.

Exercise

What do the following indicate?

(a) $\frac{3}{4}$

(b) $\frac{4}{8}$

(c) $\frac{2}{2}$

Answer

(a) 3 crotchet beats in a bar.

(b) 4 quaver beats in a bar.

(c) 2 minim beats in a bar.

The time signature of $\frac{4}{4}$ is one of the most common and we shall start our exercises with it. In fact, it is often referred to as 'common time'. As a matter of interest, you will find that in scores, an alternative to writing $\frac{4}{4}$ is sometimes used. What looks like a letter C appears instead, like this:

Actually, this symbol doesn't stand for 'common' – it's a leftover from an earlier system of rhythm notation – but that's as easy a way as any of remembering what it means. In this unit, I shall stick with $\frac{4}{4}$.

4.7 EXERCISES IN $\frac{4}{4}$

 **VIDEO NOTES
UNIT 1, VIDEO SECTION 2**

Introduction

This video section concerns the reading and playing of rhythms in $\frac{4}{4}$ time. You will need your keyboard.

In the video section, the played examples are preceded by introductory clicks to set the beat. I have used crotchets as the beat, but any note value could have been used. All the tempos are ♩ = 60.

You may need to refer back to Section 4.4 to remind yourself of the difference between a semibreve rest and a minim rest.

 NOW WATCH THE VIDEO SECTION.
YOU WILL ALSO NEED YOUR KEYBOARD.

During the video section

You are asked to play the examples below. You can use any note of the keyboard, but C is used in the video section.

Video Example 1

Video Example 2

Video Example 3

Video Example 4

After watching the video section

You should now do the exercises following these video notes.

THE EXERCISES – INITIAL ADVICE

Watching the video should have familiarized you with the basic procedure for the following exercises. The only differences are that you now need to set an underlying beat for yourself; and that you should check your success by listening to the audio-cassette.

All the exercises that follow are:

in the time signature of $\frac{4}{4}$ (four crotchet beats in every bar);

at a metronome speed of ♩ = 60, or sixty crotchet beats in a minute.

In other words the speed should be such that each crotchet or crotchet rest lasts for 1 second.

First, establish the underlying beat by tapping your foot at a speed of about one tap per second. (Complete accuracy is not essential!) You can do this by using a watch or clock – a digital model with an audible tick is ideal but anything with a second hand will serve. Continue tapping your foot to maintain the underlying beat. Now play the exercise on any note of your keyboard. Try it a few times if necessary, then listen to the cassette (Item 18) to hear if you are correct. On the cassette each model 'answer' is preceded by a complete bar of beats at ♩ = 60. Do not progress to the next exercise until you have mastered the previous one.

Incidentally, the ability to set a beat of 60 to the minute in your head is a useful skill to develop. It enables you to estimate other tempos in relation to this (e.g. ♩ = 120 is twice as fast; ♩ = 90 is one and a half times as fast).

EXERCISES WITH SEMIBREVES

Remember that a semibreve (and a semibreve rest) lasts for four crotchet beats. Thus each semibreve takes up a complete bar of $\frac{4}{4}$. Remember also that the bars are divided off from each other by bar lines; this will help your counting. You will notice that all the exercises end with a **double bar**. In musical notation this means 'The End' and always appears at the end of a

piece. It is often used to mark the end of important sections within a piece as well.

Now try the following exercises, counting each crotchet beat – aloud if you wish.

  PLAY EACH OF EXERCISES 1–3 (AS OFTEN AS YOU NEED).

LISTEN TO ITEM 18 AFTER PLAYING EACH EXERCISE.

Exercise 1

Exercise 2

Exercise 3

INTRODUCING MINIMS

The minim is half the length of a semibreve so with a $\frac{4}{4}$ time signature it lasts for two beats.

  PLAY EACH OF EXERCISES 4–6 (AS OFTEN AS YOU NEED).

LISTEN TO ITEM 18 AFTER PLAYING EACH EXERCISE.

Exercise 4

Exercise 5

Exercise 6

INTRODUCING CROTCHETS

The crotchet is half the length of a minim so it lasts for one beat. Incidentally, when you get to rests of a crotchet duration (and shorter), it's very easy to shorten them accidentally. Make sure, as you play, that the preceding note ends exactly where it should – just before the click of the beat where the rest starts. *Listen* to the silence.

  PLAY EACH OF EXERCISES 7–9 (AS OFTEN AS YOU NEED).
LISTEN TO ITEM 18 AFTER PLAYING EACH EXERCISE.

Exercise 7

Exercise 8

Exercise 9

If you are finding these exercises tiring, now would be a good moment to take a break.

INTRODUCING QUAVERS

The quaver is half the length of a crotchet so it lasts for half a crotchet beat. Thus two quavers fit into the same duration as one crotchet, and you can represent this in your counting by using the word 'and' for the second quaver of each pair: one-and-two-and-three-and-four-and.

Remember that quavers may be beamed so, for example, ♪♪ can be written ♫.

 PLAY EACH OF EXERCISES 10–12 (AS OFTEN AS YOU NEED).
LISTEN TO ITEM 18 AFTER PLAYING EACH EXERCISE.

Exercise 10

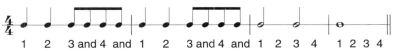

Exercise 11

Exercise 12

INTRODUCING SEMIQUAVERS

The semiquaver is half the length of a quaver, hence a quarter of the length of a crotchet. Four of them fit into the duration of one crotchet beat. You will find your finger has to be a bit sprightly when you play repeated semiquavers. There will be some advice on basic keyboard technique a little later in the course, but for the moment you just need to use the one finger, and make it work! Concentrate on fitting the notes into the right rhythmic pattern.

 PLAY EACH OF EXERCISES 13–15 (AS OFTEN AS YOU NEED).
LISTEN TO ITEM 18 AFTER PLAYING EACH EXERCISE.

Exercise 13

Exercise 14

Exercise 15

4.8 THE ANACRUSIS

All the exercises so far have started on the first beat of a bar – which is common enough in music. But what about music which does not do this? Most often, when this happens, the music starts just before the beginning of a bar, and the first note (or notes) functions as a *lead-up* to the initial strong beat. This lead-up is called an *anacrusis* – or, in the more everyday language that musicians generally use, an *upbeat* or a *pick-up*. (The term anacrusis is borrowed from poetry. In 'I wandered lonely as a cloud…' the initial, unstressed syllable, 'I', is an anacrusis.) The anacrusis is notated before the first bar-line, and, to play it, you simply have to start your beat going and fit the note(s) in the right place. Number the beats and count them to yourself: one-two-three-four. A single crotchet anacrusis will fall on 'four', thus:

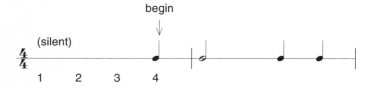

For a shorter anacrusis, you will have to count the quavers (or in rare cases the semiquavers), for example:

The silent beats before the anacrusis are not given rests.

Here are a couple of exercises with an anacrusis, or up-beat.

 PLAY EXERCISES 16 AND 17 (AS OFTEN AS YOU NEED).
LISTEN TO ITEM 18 AFTER PLAYING EACH EXERCISE.

Exercise 16

Exercise 17

4.9 DOTTED NOTES AND TIES

NOTATING MORE COMPLEX RHYTHMS

So far all the note symbols you have encountered fall into a simple system: they represent rhythmic values which are twice as long or half as long as another value. But we need to be able to notate *any* rhythm. How can we represent, say, a note lasting *three* beats? Or one and a half beats? There are two ways of doing this: using dots or using ties.

DOTTED NOTES

Dotted notes are a very widely used convention in musical notation. You will encounter these in virtually every piece you come across.

> When a **dot** is placed immediately after the head of a note (e.g. ♩. or ♪.), it increases the value of that note by exactly half its original value.

So, with a crotchet beat, a minim lasts for two beats but a dotted minim (♩.) lasts for three beats. Similarly, a dotted crotchet (♩.) lasts for one and a half beats – or to put it another way, for a duration equivalent to three quavers. It's important, by the way, that the dot comes immediately after the note; a dot below or above a note means something quite different. Dots can be added to rests as well as notes. So, for example, the dotted minim and dotted crotchet rests (▬. and ♩.) last for three beats and one and a half beats respectively, just like the equivalent notes.

Playing a dotted minim is no problem. Just count the three beats. Playing a dotted crotchet is a little more tricky. But you were introduced to the idea of counting the half-beats (one-and-two-and-three-and-four-and) in the previous section, and this is what you need to do, as, for example, in

one and two and three and four and

Dots can be applied to any note-value. But playing dotted quavers accurately (e.g.) is quite hard, and I haven't included any in the following exercises.

  PLAY EXERCISES 18 AND 19 (AS OFTEN AS YOU NEED).
LISTEN TO ITEM 18 AFTER PLAYING EACH EXERCISE.

Exercise 18

Exercise 19

THE TIE

> A **tie** (‿) or (⁀) ties together the rhythmic values of two or more adjacent notes of the same pitch.

Look at the following:

The first bar has a minim, which is two beats long, followed by a crotchet, which is one beat long – then a crotchet rest. By adding a tie to the first two notes,

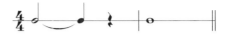

we turn them into a single note of three beats duration.

Exercise

Can you think of a different way of notating that effect?

Answer

This would give the same result:

Often a tie does exactly the same thing as a dot. Thus, as you have seen, ♩♩ = ♩. (a minim tied to a crotchet is equivalent to a dotted minim). Similarly, ♩♪ = ♩. (a crotchet tied to a quaver is equivalent to a dotted crotchet).

You have now encountered your first example of two equally legitimate ways of notating the same rhythm.

Ties are more flexible than dots. They can join together three, or even more, notes. Also, they can be used to represent durations impossible to notate using dots, for example:

But we will leave more complex rhythms of that kind for later in the course.

One final point. Although notes of any value can be tied together, rests are never tied. Instead, you must use dots, or composite sequences of rests. For example, we use ⁊· or ⁊ ⁊ but not the tied rests below:

There are conventions governing such situations, but we don't need to go into them now; you will pick them up as you go.

Here are some exercises using ties.

  PLAY EACH OF EXERCISES 20–22 (AS OFTEN AS YOU NEED). LISTEN TO ITEM 18 AFTER PLAYING EACH EXERCISE.

Exercise 20

Exercise 21

Exercise 22

4.10 OTHER SIMPLE TIME SIGNATURES

The time signature $\frac{4}{4}$ which we have been using so far is not of course the only one that is available to us. You will remember from earlier in this unit that plenty of music has two or three beats in a bar. How do we represent that? The time signature $\frac{2}{4}$ means that there are two crotchet beats in a bar. Try some exercises in this metre.

  PLAY EXERCISES 23 AND 24 (AS OFTEN AS YOU NEED). LISTEN TO ITEM 18 AFTER PLAYING EACH EXERCISE.

Exercise 23

Exercise 24

$\frac{3}{4}$ has three crotchet beats in each bar. Of course, you will tend to find plenty of dotted minims in music with this time signature.

  PLAY EACH OF EXERCISES 25–27 (AS OFTEN AS YOU NEED). LISTEN TO ITEM 18 AFTER PLAYING EACH EXERCISE.

Exercise 25

Exercise 26

Exercise 27

By the way, in $\frac{3}{4}$ and $\frac{2}{4}$ a whole bar's silence is represented, strange though it may seem, by a semibreve rest. (This is true also of other metres with fewer than four crotchets in a bar, for instance $\frac{4}{8}$ and $\frac{3}{8}$. Metres with more than four crotchets in a bar – for example, $\frac{3}{2}$ – generally use a breve rest for this purpose.) Thus in $\frac{3}{4}$ you would see the following:

not:

Illogical, admittedly, but that's how it's done.

5 SUMMARY

You have now reached the end of your first week's work. Check your progress through Section 4 by asking yourself whether you can:

1 define *time signature*;

2 recognize and write all the rhythmic symbols introduced in Sections 4.2 and 4.4 (for writing see Section 4.3);

3 describe how metronome markings work;

4 describe what dots and ties do;

5 do all the exercises – fluently.

For reference and revision purposes, it may help to know that important definitions in this unit occur in Sections 2.2, 3.3, 3.4, 3.5, 4.6 and 4.9.

ACKNOWLEDGEMENT

Figure 1   Réunion des Musées Nationaux, Service Photographique. © DACS, London, 1994.

UNIT 2

PART 1: MORE ABOUT RHYTHM
PART 2: INTRODUCING PITCH

Prepared for the Course Team by Richard Middleton and Trevor Bray

CONTENTS

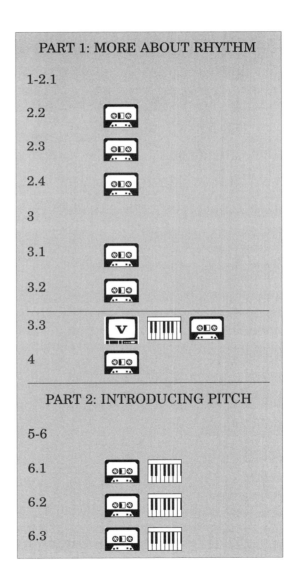

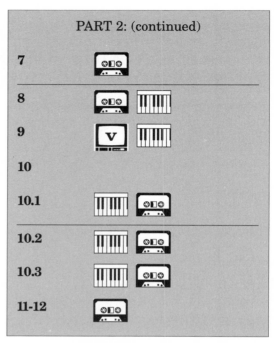

The audio items for Part 1 of this unit can be found on Audio-cassette 1.

The audio items for Part 2 of this unit can be found on Audio-cassette 2.

All the video items for this unit can be found on Video-cassette 1.

PART 1: MORE ABOUT RHYTHM

1 CONTENT AND AIMS

Part 1 of Unit 2 continues work on rhythm. The aims set out in Unit 1 Section 1 continue to apply. This work should occupy rather less than half of your week. Part 2 of Unit 2 then introduces you to the element of pitch.

In addition to your keyboard, Video-cassette 1, Audio-cassette 1 and your video- and audio-cassette players, you will need some manuscript paper (for Section 12).

Having spent the last few days on a lot of concocted exercises, you may well be ready for a return to real music. So I start Part 1 with a section focused on listening rather than notation. Really this section (Section 2) is a bit of a digression, since it's not essential for your progress on the course. However, the subject – irregular metres – is of considerable interest, and it will broaden your knowledge and deepen your perception of rhythm. But if you struggled with Unit 1, or if you find time pressing, you are quite at liberty to scan through Section 2 fairly quickly. You can always come back to it later. And, don't worry too much if you find it hard going.

2 IRREGULAR METRES

2.1 INTRODUCTION

Back in Unit 1 Section 3.3, I pointed out that the phenomenon of a *beat* in music could perhaps be linked to processes marked by regularly recurring patterns elsewhere: day and night; heart-beat; walking, and so on. But in such processes the pattern is not always *absolutely* regular. Days and nights vary in length – but we still recognize in them a certain predictability. Meal-time rhythms survive even if lunch is an hour late. Listen to your heat-beat or breathing: is it mechanically even? So we might wonder if musical beat is always absolutely regular.

2.2 MUSIC WITH AN IRREGULAR BEAT

Audio-cassette Item 1 consists of three parts. First (Item 1a) there's that old friend you first heard as Item 8 in Unit 1: a totally regular beat (think of it as

crotchets) with an even flow of shorter notes (quavers) against it. I can now give a notated form of this:

Example 1

Then (Item 1b) you hear the flow of quavers continuing but the beat pattern changes. It's no longer regular; the notes aren't all the same length. And thirdly (Item 1c), you hear a longer passage in which the first two alternate.

Exercise

LISTEN NOW TO ITEMS 1(a), 1(b) AND 1(c).

(a) Can you describe what happens to the beat in Item 1(b)?

(b) When you are confident you can hear the difference between Item 1(a) and Item 1(b), try clapping the beat in Item 1(c), changing the pattern of your claps in line with the music.

Discussion

(a) Some of the beats stay the same length as in Item 1(a) but others are lengthened by fifty per cent. To put it another way, some have two quavers against them but others now have three:

Example 2

So we would have to notate these longer beats as dotted crotchets.

(b) You would only have been able to do this reliably and accurately if you realised that the alternations of long and short beats in Item 1(b) fall into a regular pattern. The pattern of beat-lengths runs long-long-short; or, to put it in terms of quavers, 3 + 3 + 2, as in Example 3.

Example 3

If you didn't hear that, listen again to Item 1(b) and then try the clapping exercise to Item 1(c) once more.

This 3 + 3 + 2 pattern is very common in Africa and South America, and crops up in Afro-American music too. You can see that, because it recurs consistently, it forms a metrical group (marked by bar-lines in the example above). In fact, each group occupies the equivalent of four crotchets (3 + 3 + 2 = 8 quavers = 4 crotchets). But it would be odd to give it a time-signature of $\frac{4}{4}$ because there is no regular crotchet beat. Since the beat is not regular, metres of this sort are termed **irregular metres**.

2.3 SOME EXAMPLES

Now let's listen to a real piece which uses the 3 + 3 + 2 pattern. It's an Afro-American dance-song – though the techniques could be traced to African antecedents.

The 3 + 3 + 2 pattern is played on the bass drum. Concentrate on that and try to clap with it. Snare drum and fife have more complex rhythmic patterns over the top. There's also hand-clapping, and you might try to join in with that. In relation to the bass drum, the hand-clapping runs like this:

Example 4

 LISTEN NOW TO ITEM 2.

Now try a similar, but I think rather harder, exercise with Item 3. This piece has an irregular metre, but it is not 3 + 3 + 2.

Exercise

 LISTEN NOW TO ITEM 3.

Can you describe the metre? Use words (such as long–long–short), or notation.

Discussion

That was difficult and you shouldn't feel too down-hearted if you couldn't do it. The pattern is short-short-long and could be notated as:

Example 5

You can see that there are seven quavers in each bar. This pattern is common in various East European folk musics, which were a significant influence on the composer of this piece, Béla Bartók.

Figure 1   Béla Bartók (1881–1945). Hungarian composer, pianist and authority on folk music. Photographed in 1936 by Kata Kalman.

2.4 ADDITIVE METRES AND THEIR TIME SIGNATURES

Another term for these irregular metres is **additive** – because each metrical group is made up by adding together beats of more than a single duration. By contrast, metres with a regular beat ($\frac{2}{4}$, $\frac{3}{4}$, $\frac{4}{4}$, for example) are called **multiplicative**, or **divisive**: the relationship between beat and bar is one of simple multiplication (or looking at it the other way round, of simple division).

Most European music – certainly almost all the music you will study in this course – has a regular beat and a multiplicative metre. Additive metres, though, have become more common in twentieth-century music, not only in Bartók but also Stravinsky and many other composers. I can't resist adding too that even in regular-beat music good performers rarely play the beats absolutely evenly. The waltz, though clearly in $\frac{3}{4}$ time, gives us a striking example of this, for in the Viennese performing tradition the second beat in each bar is brought forward very slightly and given an extra accent – not enough to make us doubt that the metre is regular but enough to distort the mathematical precision.

 LISTEN TO THIS EFFECT IN ITEM 4.

One final point before we return to more straightforward metres. What time signatures would we give music with 3 + 3 + 2 or 2 + 2 + 3 metres? Well, 3 + 3 + 2 is often described as $\frac{8}{8}$ – or, if more precision is required, $\frac{3+3+2}{8}$.

Bartók's 2 + 2 + 3 pattern can be shown as $\frac{7}{8}$, or perhaps $\frac{2+2+3}{8}$.

You can see that the principle behind these time signatures is different from that governing those we met earlier ($\frac{2}{4}$, $\frac{3}{4}$, $\frac{4}{4}$). In additive metres, the lower number in the time signature no longer tells us which note-value represents the beat; instead, it simply indicates a particular rhythmic value (in this case, quavers) which the upper number is then going to add up, giving us the total number making up one bar.

There are two general lessons to be drawn from this section:

1 It is possible to divide a beat into three equal parts rather than into two.

2 Sometimes time signatures show not the number and type of beats in a bar but rather the number of a particular, convenient rhythmic value.

Both these points will be important in the next section.

3 COMPOUND METRES

3.1 DIVIDING THE BEAT INTO THREE

Let me repeat the first of those conclusions, set out at the end of Section 2. It is possible to divide a beat into three equal parts rather than into two. You met this principle in the course of your excursion into irregular metres. Now I'm going to approach it again but from a different angle.

Item 5 harks back to the demonstrations of beat and metre you worked on in Unit 1 (Audio-cassette 1 Items 8 and 11). This time a regular beat is established, then joined by quicker notes which divide each beat into two. So far, so familiar. But then you will hear the quicker notes speed up slightly so that they divide the beat into *three*. The tempo and beat stay the same; it's just the division of the beat that alters. Concentrate on the moment when groups of two give way to groups of three, and get familiar with the difference.

 LISTEN NOW TO ITEM 5.

If we think of the beat as a crotchet, the groups of two quicker notes are quavers of course:

Example 6

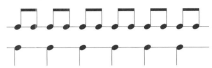

The easiest way to notate the groups of three quicker notes would be to use quavers for them too – but then the beat would logically have to be written as a dotted crotchet; it contains three quavers:

Example 7

Notice, by the way, how (as I described in Unit 1 Section 4.3) the beaming of the quavers follows the beat structure. In notation, the moment of changeover from groups of two quavers to groups of three, would look like this:

Example 8

The sign ♩ = ♩. means that after the double bar a dotted crotchet is the same duration as a crotchet was before the double bar.

I might add that if the change from two-quaver groups to three-quaver groups were temporary, there is a way of notating it without switching to dotted crotchets. We could use *triplets*, like this:

Example 9

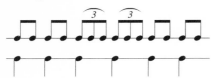

A **triplet** is a group of three notes to be performed in the time of two of the same kind.

As you can see, triplets are indicated by the figure three, with – usually – a slur (which is the curved line placed above the 3 numeral in Example 9).

Triplets would be a cumbersome method of notation for whole pieces or long stretches of music where the beat was divided into threes throughout. In such cases, as I said, we use a dotted-note beat.

Let's listen to another example of a transition from a crotchet to a dotted-crotchet beat. The next item on the audio-cassette contains a changeover similar to the one in Item 5 but this time in a real piece of music. There are two tunes. The first is in ⁴⁄₄ at a moderate tempo (♩ = 108 approximately). There are lots of quavers in the tune and it's easy to count one-and-two-and-three-and-four-and to it. This gives way to a second tune, a jig. The tempo

stays the same but, as in all jigs, the beat is now divided not into two quavers but three. It's a bit fast to count one-and-and-two-and-and-three-and-and (there are three beats to the bar in this jig) but you can probably manage something like one-a-a-two-a-a-three-a-a: anything to help you feel the groups of three quavers. You will hear me counting at times during these tunes to give you some help.

 LISTEN NOW TO ITEM 6.

I hope you found no great difficulty with that. Try another, similar exercise.

Exercise

Item 7, like the previous piece, divides into two parts. In one the beat divides into twos, whereas in the other it divides into threes. Which is which?

 LISTEN NOW TO ITEM 7.

Discussion

This time the threes come first, the twos second. (There are two tunes in each part.) In this piece the tempo does not stay the same over the change of rhythm. Nevertheless, I think the difference is clear. If you found it unclear, try putting nonsense syllables to the rhythms. You will find that did-dle-di did-dle-di (i.e. 1–2–3, 1–2–3) goes well to the groups of three, and did-dle did-dle (i.e. 1–2, 1–2) goes to the groups of two. This may help you to hear the groupings.

3.2 COMPOUND TIME SIGNATURES

The rhythm of the jig you heard in Item 6 looks like this:

Example 10

 etc.

What time signature should it have? There are three beats in a bar but we can't say it's in ³⁄₄ because the beat is not a crotchet. This metre is described as $\frac{9}{8}$. You can see that, in terms of the principles governing $\frac{2}{4}$, $\frac{3}{4}$ and $\frac{4}{4}$, this time signature is misleading. In $\frac{9}{8}$ there are not nine beats in a bar, nor is the beat a quaver. Although there is a regular mathematical principle behind all time signatures, the simplest way to get to grips with $\frac{9}{8}$ and others like it – which are called **compound** time signatures – is just to *learn* them.

> Metres which divide the beat into twos are called **simple**. Metres which divide the beat into threes are called **compound**.

In compound time signatures, the top figures 6, 9 and 12 mean two, three and four beats in a bar respectively; the lower figures 4, 8 and 16 mean that the beat is a dotted minim, a dotted crotchet and a dotted quaver respectively. Don't worry too much about dotted minim and dotted quaver beats for now; you won't come across them very often. The most common compound time signatures are $\frac{6}{8}$, $\frac{9}{8}$ and $\frac{12}{8}$, and they are the equivalent of $\frac{2}{4}$, $\frac{3}{4}$ and $\frac{4}{4}$, respectively, as shown below.

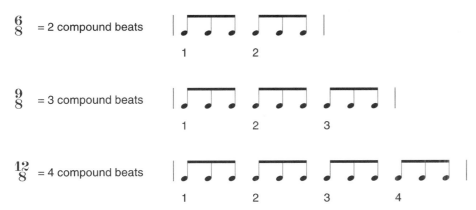

A rule of thumb is that whenever the upper number is a multiple of three, the time signature is a compound one.

Exercise

> Listen again to the first part (the part in compound metre) of Item 7. The two tunes have two different time signatures. Can you hear how many beats in a bar each tune has? Are there two, three or four?

Discussion

The first has two beats to a bar; it's in $\frac{6}{8}$. The second tune has three beats to a bar; it's in $\frac{9}{8}$. You may have found this difficult to spot at first. If so, concentrate on the phrase structure (a **phrase** in music is roughly the equivalent of a verbal phrase). The phrases are two bars long, and each starts on a strong beat. This will help you to hear the patterns of accents, and you will find it's impossible for the first tune to be regarded as 'in three', or the second as 'in two'.

Obviously, in compound metres, notes longer than quavers will often be dotted. Here is a chart of common relationships between rhythmic values, found in $\frac{6}{8}$, $\frac{9}{8}$ and $\frac{12}{8}$. It will be useful for reference.

3.3   EXERCISES IN COMPOUND TIME

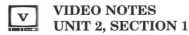 **VIDEO NOTES
UNIT 2, SECTION 1**

Introduction

This video section concerns the reading and playing of rhythms in compound time. You will need your keyboard.

In the video section, the played examples are preceded by introductory clicks to set the beat. In compound time the beat is always a dotted note.

I have used dotted crotchets as the beat, but any dotted note value could have been used. All the tempos are ♩. = 60.

 NOW WATCH THE VIDEO SECTION.
YOU WILL ALSO NEED YOUR KEYBOARD.

During the video section

You see and hear the following examples of ⁶⁄₈ rhythms.

Video Example 1

Video Example 2

Video Example 3

After watching the video section

You should now do the exercises following these video notes.

THE EXERCISES – INITIAL ADVICE

As in the equivalent exercises in Unit 1, set a tempo of about sixty beats per minute. In the following exercises, of course, the beat will be a dotted crotchet. Set your foot tapping at this tempo, then play the exercise on any note on your keyboard. Try it a few times if necessary, then listen to the audio-cassette to hear whether you are correct. As before, on the audio-cassette each 'answer' is preceded by a complete bar of beats at ♩. = 60. Do not progress to the next exercise until you have mastered the previous one.

EXERCISES IN ⁶⁄₈; TWO DOTTED CROTCHET BEATS IN A BAR

 PLAY EXERCISE 1.
 LISTEN TO ITEM 8.

Exercise 1

I hope you remembered that in compound time ♩. represents *two* beats. In ⁶⁄₈, therefore, it fills a whole bar. In addition to ♩. and ♫, a common pattern for a single beat in compound time is ♩♪ and this will be introduced in the following exercises. Remember that a crotchet (♩) will not be worth 'one' – that is, it will not be a complete single beat.

 PLAY EXERCISES 2 AND 3.
 LISTEN TO ITEM 8 AFTER EACH EXERCISE.

Exercise 2

Exercise 3

EXERCISES IN 9/8; THREE DOTTED CROTCHET BEATS IN A BAR

9/8 is the compound equivalent of 3/4. There are three beats in each bar. Don't forget that ♩. represents two beats; so ♩. ♩. represents three beats – a whole bar in this metre.

PLAY EACH OF EXERCISES 4–6.

LISTEN TO ITEM 8 AFTER EACH EXERCISE.

Exercise 4

Exercise 5

Exercise 6

EXERCISES IN 12/8; FOUR DOTTED CROTCHET BEATS IN A BAR

12/8 is the compound equivalent of 4/4. There are four beats in each bar. How would we write a note that would fill up a whole bar? If you work it out, you will find you need a dotted semibreve (= 12 quavers).

PLAY EACH OF EXERCISES 7–9.

LISTEN TO ITEM 8 AFTER EACH EXERCISE.

Exercise 7

Exercise 8

Exercise 9

4   AURAL TRAINING

I hope that you feel you are now moving towards a reasonably good grasp of the relationship between rhythmic symbols on the page and the rhythmic patterns you hear. There may be some problems and blind (or deaf) spots; but if you have mastered the basic principles, you should be content: *all* music involves rhythm, so your subsequent work throughout the course can't help but improve your understanding bit by bit. A good way to both check your progress and improve it is to try some aural dictation tests. These reverse the procedure followed in the exercises you have done up to now. Instead of being asked to play rhythms that are given to you in notation, you are asked to listen to rhythms on the cassette, write them down, and then check whether they are correct.

You will need this unit, some sheets of ruled paper and audio-cassette Item 9. Listen to one test at a time. For each test you will hear:

1   An announcement of the test number (e.g. Aural Test no. 1).

2   An announcement of the time signature for the test.

3   Two bars' worth of introductory beats to give you the tempo.

4   The test itself. It will begin on the first beat of a bar.

5   The introductory beats and the test again.

6   The announcement 'now check your answer against that in the unit'.

The 'answers' are to be found at the back of this unit. Obviously you should resist the temptation to look at them before you have tried hard to notate a particular test yourself.

Basically there are two methods of taking down music from dictation (or, when you come to real music, from performance). You can notate as you listen; or you can listen, remember, then notate from memory. The first method requires your hand to keep up with the sounds, so just write the note-heads, plus, perhaps, any dots and the barlines; you can probably invent a shorthand for any rests. The following example:

in an initial attempt, using a shorthand, might look like Figure 2.

Figure 2

You would need to *remember* that the fourth note was a quaver. And indeed, you might find that a mixture of the two methods – real-time notation *and* memory – works best (I do myself). For example, as you listen, you could just make marks to represent each note, spacing them out in a rough representation of their relative durations as in Figure 3.

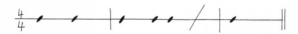

Figure 3

Then, using this as a mnemonic, you would fill in the details from memory. And then you could check your memory from a second hearing.

I recommend that you experiment with different methods. What suits one person doesn't necessarily suit another. If you get stuck, don't despair. Put the tests aside, come back to them a day or two later, and you may well find your abilities have improved in the meantime.

 NOW TRY THE AURAL TESTS IN ITEM 9.
ANSWERS ARE AT THE END OF THE UNIT (P. 47).

CHECKPOINT

This completes your initial work on rhythm. Your knowledge will increase as you proceed through the course. As a check on your work so far in Unit 2, ask yourself whether you

1   understand what irregular metres are (this is a desirable but not essential objective);

2   can describe the difference between simple and compound time signatures;

3   can do the exercises in Section 3.3;

4   can do the aural tests in Section 4.

PART 2: INTRODUCING PITCH

5 CONTENT AND AIMS

So far during the course you have been studying rhythm. This is perhaps the most fundamental characteristic of music as Donald Burrows demonstrated in the Course Introduction, where he compared the Schubert theme firstly devoid of rhythm and then pitch. The latter was more easily recognizable. Nonetheless, pitch has a very important part to play in music, and in the second part of this unit you will be introduced to some basic facts about it as well as to some concepts related to pitch, notably the scale, the (musical) interval, and a particular interval, the octave. There is also a plentiful supply of aural exercises relating to basic characteristics of pitch for you to work, and these will help you to:

1 distinguish aurally between notes that are higher or lower than others and some that are the same;

2 recognize the interval of an octave;

3 identify the lower of two notes sounding together.

Note that in some of these exercises you will be asked to sing certain pitches either out loud or in your head. Basically, then, this half of the unit concentrates on pitch, and we shall begin by trying to define what pitch is.

The audio items for this part of the unit are on Audio-cassette 2.

6 TOWARDS A DEFINITION OF PITCH

6.1 DEFINITE AND INDEFINITE PITCH

Turn to Item 10 on the audio-cassette. This consists of a succession of seven separate sounds played on different instruments. Listen to the sounds carefully, bearing the following questions in mind:

1 Is it possible to describe any of these sounds as lacking in pitch? Are they pitchless, so to speak?

2 Can you match the pitch of each sound by singing or humming the note?

3 If you can't match some of the sounds, which ones are they? Notice that each sound will be played twice, and if you have trouble matching the different sounds by singing or humming, try matching them with a note played on your keyboard.

LISTEN NOW TO ITEM 10.

There are two possible responses to the first question above. The most likely response would be to consider that some of the sounds have pitch but that others do not. And, by attempting to match the pitches by singing or playing the relevant note, you might have suggested for the third question that sounds 1, 2 and 5 could be matched but the rest could not. Sounds 1, 2 and 5 were in fact produced respectively on a piano, a clarinet and a cello. The others, the ones that could not be matched, were played on a triangle (3), bass drum (4), side drum (6) and cymbal (7). Listen to the sounds again, following Table 1.

Table 1

Sounds that can be matched	Sounds that cannot be matched
1　piano	3　triangle
2　clarinet	4　bass drum
5　cello	6　side drum
	7　cymbal

Figure 4　A clarinet (a woodwind instrument).

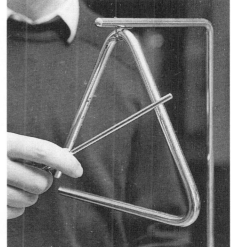

Figure 5　A triangle, played by striking with a metal beater.

Another response to the first question would be to consider that *all* the sounds have some sort of pitch. The sounds in the first group, 1 (piano), 2 (clarinet) and 5 (cello), can be described as high, low or middling. The piano was middling, the clarinet higher and the cello lower. But then so too can the sounds of the second group. For instance, sound 4, the bass drum, sounds lower than sound 6, the side drum; the triangle, sound 3, like the side drum, has a relatively higher pitch than the bass drum. Thus both groups have a pitch element. Nonetheless, despite this similarity, the two groups are fundamentally different. The sounds of the first group have a precise, definite pitch that can be matched by humming or playing a note yourself, whereas those in the second group are less precise, and are called indefinite in pitch. These pitches are impossible to locate exactly.

During the twentieth century, many composers both in Europe and America have been fascinated by the contrast between definite and indefinite pitches. Indeed some have written pieces that rely almost entirely on indefinite pitches. One of the earliest of these pieces, *Ionisation* (1931), was written by the French composer Edgard Varèse (1883–1965). Since it is the percussion section of the orchestra that produces the greatest variety of indefinite pitches – and our second group of instruments, triangle, bass drum, side drum and cymbal, all belong to this section – Varèse chose over 30 different percussion instruments for his piece. The idea of contrasting the higher- medium- and lower-sounding percussion instruments is one of the features of *Ionisation* and at the beginning, as you can hear as audio-cassette Item 11, Varèse concentrates on the higher-sounding instruments. Following a (28-second) introduction, the main rhythmic idea comes on a variety of the side drum.

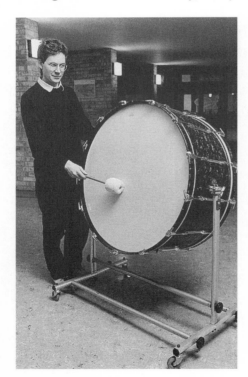

Figure 6   A bass drum. Struck with a felt-headed stick, using the free hand to dampen the sound.

Figure 7   A cello (pronounced 'chello'). The player draws a bow, in the right hand, across the strings.

Figure 8   A side drum (or snare drum). The drummer strikes it with a pair of wooden sticks.

Figure 9   A suspended cymbal. The player strikes it with wooden or felt-headed sticks.

LISTEN NOW TO ITEM 11.

6.2   HIGH AND LOW

While discussing the contrast between definite and indefinite pitches we have already suggested that pitches can be high or low, and indeed the concept of the highness and lowness of pitch is one that develops in us from birth. We differentiate between our mother's and father's voices by, among other things, their pitch; we soon come to notice the changing pitch of the wind whistling through the trees or telephone wires. Other pitches we hear are more definite – the alternating pitch of a two-tone door-bell, the beep of an electronic watch, and so on. Several natural phenomena exhibit a much more complex use of different pitches both definite and indefinite, such as bird-song, but the most easily recognizable bird-song is one of the simplest, that of the cuckoo. Only two pitches are produced, but the fundamental fact about them is that the first is higher than the second. This pattern – higher pitch followed by lower pitch – is so significant that if it were reversed we wouldn't think we were listening to a cuckoo but to a friend playing a practical joke on us! Recognition of the pattern is crucial. Some composers, eager to populate their nature pieces with birds, have seized on this fact, and whatever other birds they might attempt to imitate in their music, the cuckoo's call is unmistakable. In audio-cassette Items 12 and 13, you'll hear two cuckoos, the first coming at the end of the slow movement of Beethoven's Sixth Symphony, the *Pastoral* (1808), and the second calling distantly in a piece composed just over a hundred years later, Delius's *On Hearing the First Cuckoo in Spring* (1912).

 LISTEN NOW TO ITEMS 12 AND 13.

> The distance in pitch between the higher and lower note (or the lower and higher) is called **an interval** in musical terminology.

We shall return to the subject of intervals during Sections 7 and 10 of this part of the unit in preparation for an extended discussion of the concept in Units 4 and 6.

6.3   HOW IS A DEFINITE PITCH PRODUCED?

So far, in pursuit of a definition of pitch, we have discovered two of pitch's basic characteristics:

1   it can be definite or indefinite;

2   it can have highness or lowness.

But how is this highness and lowness produced and transmitted? What makes a pitch high or low?

Sounds are transmitted by tiny changes in air pressure. For example, if two hard surfaces collide, a sound is produced by the air being forced out from between the surfaces – the air pressure increases. Following this increase, the pressure decreases, usually overshooting the mark, producing a decrease in air pressure. After a few oscillations, the air pressure returns to normal. If this pattern is repeated but in a random fashion, noise will result. However, as soon as the pattern is repeated regularly a note with a specific pitch is produced. The slower the regular repetitions, the lower the note; the quicker the regular repetitions, the higher the note. You can hear this if we undertake a simple experiment. Listen to audio-cassette Item 14. First of all you will hear a few isolated clicks. Gradually, the clicks will be speeded up. At the point of roughly 20 clicks per second you will begin to hear a low pitch and as the clicks speed up further the pitch will rise higher and higher.

 LISTEN NOW TO ITEM 14.

So definite pitches are transmitted by the regular repetition of changes in air pressure. Moreover, the way the regular repeated changes are produced does not affect the principle. The changes of air pressure might result from blowing into a single reed (as in the clarinet, Figures 4 and 10) which causes a column of air to vibrate, or by bowing a taut string (as in the violin) to make it vibrate. The principle is the same. If the vibrations cause regular changes of air pressure, then definite pitches will be produced. The more rapid these vibrations, the more rapid will be the regular changes of air pressure; hence the higher will be the pitch. The slower the vibrations, the lower the pitch.

The speed at which a cycle of these regular changes of air pressure occurs is called **frequency**, and one cycle of, for instance, a vibrating string would consist initially of the string's maximum displacement in one direction away from its normal resting point, the mid-position; then the movement back to

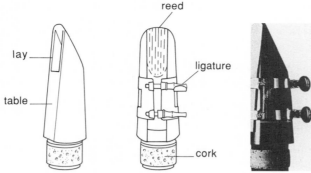

Figure 10(a)   Two views of a clarinet reed. Reeds are made from cane or plastic.

Figure 10(b)   A clarinet mouthpiece to which the reed is clamped at one end by the ligature (the metal band). The other end of the cane is free to vibrate when the player blows through the mouthpiece.

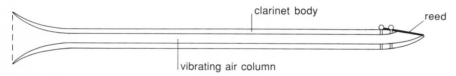

Figure 10(c)   A vibrating column of air is created within the clarinet body when the reed in the mouthpiece vibrates.

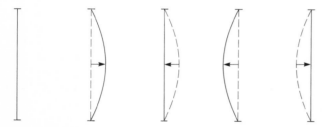

Figure 11   One cycle of a vibrating string

the mid-position and on out to the maximum displacement in the opposite direction; and finally back to the mid position (Figure 11).

Frequency is measured in cycles per second or hertz (defined below). For example, the note A, played on the oboe when an orchestra is tuning up, usually has a frequency of 440 cycles per second or hertz. (When you come to

Section 8 of this unit, you will realize why 'A' might not necessarily be of the frequency 440 hertz, but a different figure instead.)

We can now attempt a working definition for pitch:

Pitch is of two types, indefinite and definite. **Indefinite pitch** is produced by a vibrating source that causes random changes of air pressure. **Definite pitch** is produced by a vibrating source that causes regular changes of air pressure. The frequency of a particular pitch is measured in cycles per second or hertz. A low frequency is produced when there are slower regular changes of air pressure; a high frequency by more rapid regular changes.

CHECKPOINT

Make sure that you understand this definition before proceeding further, and if necessary re-read those parts of the text you have not grasped. Incidentally, the name hertz (often abbreviated to Hz) is used as the label for a unit of frequency in homage to the German physicist, Heinrich Hertz (1857–94), whose researches made radio, television and radar possible.

7   SOME PRACTICAL WORK (I)

We have seen that a higher note followed by a lower note is characteristic of a cuckoo's song; and an ability to recognize this pitch pattern is necessary for spotting cuckoos both in the wild and in musical surroundings. A cuckoo is differentiated from other birds by the particular pattern of its song. Similarly, if one is trying to differentiate between different tunes, recognition of the tunes' shapes, with their highs and lows, ups and downs, is essential. So let us begin, simply, by attempting to recognize highness and lowness in pairs of successive notes.

Exercise 10

If you listen to audio-cassette Item 15, you will hear ten pairs of notes. The first note will be either higher or lower than the second; please state which. In two of the pairs, the notes will be at the same pitch.

The answers can be found at the back of the unit.

LISTEN NOW TO ITEM 15.

Discussion

If you found difficulty with any of these pairs, please listen again several times now that you know the correct answers. It is only by listening repeatedly to the sounds that you will improve your success rate. As with the aural exercises on rhythm that you have already done, and the many more that will follow during the course, there is no reason why you should achieve a 100 per cent correct result at the first go. Admittedly the ear, like any other part of the body, has a certain natural facility, and this innate ability varies from person to person. However, very few of us have such a brilliant ear as, for instance, Mozart, who at the age of 14 wrote out the score of Allegri's *Miserere* after only one hearing. At the same time, very few of us have little or no facility (i.e. are 'tone-deaf'). So regular practice is essential if we want to improve our ability to recognize given sounds. Just as physical fitness can only be achieved through daily regular exercise, so too the ear has to be trained. And the best way to do this is not to undertake a long, tiring session once in a while, but to practise for a little time as often as possible.

The distance between the pairs of high and low pitches you heard just now – that is, the interval – was very large. In the next exercise smaller intervals will be chosen, and these are, for many people, more difficult to distinguish. However, before we take our leave of very large intervals, listen to audio-cassette Item 16, which contains a further four pairs of pitches. The lower note will come first in each case.

 LISTEN NOW TO ITEM 16.

These pairs consist of the bottom and top notes of
   the piano,
   the cello,
   the violin,
   the clarinet.

These pitches define the limits of the **range** of pitches available from these instruments,[1] and if you refer to Figure 12, you can see, diagrammatically,

how these ranges relate to one another, and indeed how they relate to that of a piano and of a 5-octave electronic keyboard. Notice, too, how these ranges relate to the range of frequencies audible to the human ear. This extends from roughly 20 hertz at the bottom of the range to about 20,000 hertz (or 20 kHz) at the top. This range varies from person to person and, as we get older, contracts. The optimum range occurs at the age of 16, and a 60-year-old can hear only up to about 10 kHz at the top end of the range.

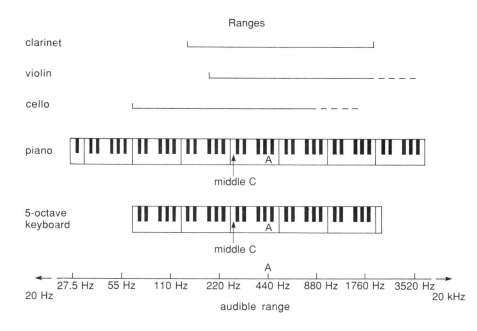

Figure 12   Pitch ranges of a few instruments in relation to the audible range of pitches.

Exercise 11

Item 17 contains another ten pairs of pitches, but with the pitches closer together. Is the first pitch higher or lower than the second? As in the previous exercise, two of the pairs will contain a repeated pitch. Answers can be found at the back of the unit.

[1]In practice, the upper limit of the range is not fixed for stringed instruments, and even the piano can have additional notes added at both the upper and lower ends of the range.

NOW LISTEN TO ITEM 17.

Discussion

As with the previous exercise, practice makes perfect, so, bearing the correct answers in mind, listen again to Item 17 several times if you had any of the answers wrong. Incidentally, with the pairs of pitches numbered 7, 8 and 10, the notes were very close together and could well have caused you difficulty. But perseverance with listening should sort things out.

CHECKPOINT

You have now had some practice at recognizing that some notes are higher or lower than others (see Section 5, first aim), and should be making some headway with this particular skill.

8 A HISTORICAL PERSPECTIVE

During Section 6.3, when discussing how definite pitches are produced, I noted that the pitch used for tuning up an orchestra was that of a particular frequency, 440 hertz. This is the standard frequency for the note A, stipulated at the British Standards Institution Conference of 1938, and reaffirmed by the International Organization for Standardization in 1955 and 1975. Since the standard of A = 440 hertz has been in use for some time, and the avid concert-goer will have become accustomed to this particular frequency from hearing orchestras tune up to it so frequently, the fixing of the pitch A at 440 hertz might appear immutable. However, this is far from the case both nowadays and in musical history. Indeed at certain times in the past, pitch-levels have varied significantly from the present standard, and some of these variants are included in Table 2. The table runs from the highest pitch for A at the top, to the lowest at the bottom.

In Table 2, the second column from the left lists several different pitch-levels for the note A, with the standard of 440 hertz as level 3, and the others ranging from around 480 hertz (pitch-level 1) to roughly 360 hertz (pitch-level 7). The letter *c* before some pitch-levels (standing for the Latin *circa*) means 'about' and indicates that the frequencies are approximate.

This range is highly significant since it either raises or lowers the note A a considerable amount. You can appreciate this by playing the following notes on your piano or keyboard. First of all find the note A by referring to Figure 12. This shows the whereabouts of this note on both a modern 7-octave piano and a 5-octave electronic keyboard. Notice that the black notes are arranged in groups of two and three along the keyboard. The note A is the one that comes between the second and third black notes in the three-black-note group.

Table 2 Performing pitch-levels

Pitch-level of A	Date	Example
1 A = *c.* 480 Hz	1684–5	Durham Cathedral organ (A = 474)
	First half of eighteenth century	Pitch for many organs at Leipzig, Weimar and Hamburg in Bach's time
2 A = *c.* 455 Hz	Late nineteenth century	Orchestral pitch in London, New York and Vienna
3 A = 440 Hz	1938	British Standards Institution Conference
4 A = *c.* 430 Hz	1698	Ordinary French orchestral pitch
	1740	Tuning fork associated with Handel in London (A = 422.5)
	1780	Stein's tuning fork (A = 421.5)
	1813	London Philharmonic fork (A = 423.5)
	1859	French government standard (A = 435)
5 A = *c.* 410 Hz	1670s–80s	Lully's opera pitch in France
6 A = *c.* 380 Hz	First half of eighteenth century	French organ pitch
7 A = *c.* 360 Hz	1611	Worcester Cathedral organ

If your piano or keyboard has been tuned to modern standard concert pitch, this note should have the frequency 440 hertz. Now the *black* note to the *right* of A has a frequency of about 466 hertz and, as you can see from the table, this lies between levels 1 and 2. Therefore, pitch-level 2 sounds a little lower in pitch than this black note, but pitch-level 1 sounds a little higher. Thus when pitch-levels 1 and 2 were used, the note A was not the note A on your piano or keyboard, but closer to the black note on the right of A.

With the *black* note to the *left* of A sounding at about 415 hertz and the *white* note to the *left* of A sounding at about 392 hertz, you can judge the rough pitches of A for the other pitch-levels. For instance, with the tuning fork associated with Handel sounding at A = 422.5 Hz, this pitch-level is much closer to the black note to the left of A on your keyboard than to A itself. Figure 13 summarizes these pitch relationships.

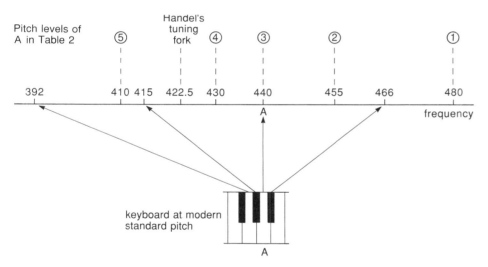

Figure 13   Pitch levels of Table 2 in relation to a keyboard at modern standard pitch (A = 440 Hz).

Pitch-levels have varied considerably, then, and the details of the pitch-levels of organs provide interesting evidence of this. Two organs built in England during the seventeenth century, one at Worcester in 1611, the other at Durham in 1684–5, were tuned with very different pitch-levels for A. Similarly, during the early eighteenth century, the pitch-level of German organs was significantly different from that of French organs, reflecting different traditions. Now, consider orchestral pitch-levels. Is there a particular trend noticeable from the late seventeenth century to the present? For instance, does the pitch-level gradually fall, gradually rise, remain stable, or what?

Table 2 shows that, despite the fact that Lully adopted a lower pitch-level for the performance of his operas than that used for orchestral performance in France at the time, there was a consensus of opinion, lasting roughly 150 years, that the note A should be approximately 430 hertz. Tuning forks associated with Handel in London, Stein (whose Viennese pianos were known to Mozart) and the Philharmonic Society in London all produce pitches around the 422/3 hertz mark, and in 1859 the French government fixed the standard pitch-level for A at 435 hertz. However, by the late nineteenth century, the pitch-level had risen to *c*. 455 hertz. This was reduced to 440 hertz at the British Standards Institution Conference in 1938.

Of course setting a standard pitch-level is one thing; adopting it is another. Orchestras nowadays do not necessarily comply with the standard. In practice, some orchestras prefer a slightly higher pitch-level because, it is felt, this adjustment adds a brightness to the sound. The current interest in performing music in a manner close to the original performing practice has also undermined the idea of a set, standard pitch-level since the pitch-levels that existed for the original performances are often used in preference to the present standard. Listen now to audio-cassette Items 18 and 19. These consist of two performances of the opening of Handel's *Messiah* with different pitch-levels, the latter being one that reflects that of the original performance practice. How do the different pitch-levels affect the music? Is the overall expressive effect the same in both performances?

 LISTEN NOW TO ITEMS 18 AND 19.

To a certain extent the expressive effect is similar in both performances. One could hardly expect a vast change to have occurred simply because the pitch-level had been lowered somewhat. Nonetheless, the second recording sounds overall less bright and aggressive. This is not entirely due to the adoption of a lower pitch-level. Other factors are involved: construction, for instance. The old-style violins on the second recording use gut strings, whereas modern instruments use wire. Gut gives a less penetrating sound. In addition, the playing techniques used on the older instruments do not permit such a bright, aggressive attack as can be obtained on their modern equivalent. But the lower pitch-level certainly contributes to the more mellow, and indeed, refined, effect.

Needless to say, this discussion of pitch-levels has been necessarily brief; it is a large, complex subject with many ramifications, particularly for the performer. But the main point to remember is that *pitch-levels have varied from time to time and place to place*. Even personal preference can dictate the setting of the pitch-level used in a performance. Some attempts at standardization have been made, but, in practice, the standard pitch-level chosen is not always suitable for all musical contexts. Pitch-levels have varied considerably and doubtless will continue to do so.

9 STARTING AT THE KEYBOARD

 VIDEO NOTES
UNIT 2, VIDEO SECTION 2

Introduction

This video section consists of an introduction to your keyboard and is really aimed at complete beginners. If you have some expertise at playing a keyboard instrument, then you might like to omit this discussion and pass straight on to Section 10.

Before watching the video section

You should be seated at your keyboard for this video section. Try to sit so that your lower arm, wrist and hand are roughly horizontal when your hands are resting on the notes of the keyboard. If they slope downwards slightly, that's fine; but avoid sitting so low that they rise up to the keyboard. Such a position would soon tire your wrists. Your arms and hands should be relaxed, not stiff. If you prefer to use a chair with a back, that's quite acceptable.

 NOW WATCH THE VIDEO SECTION.
YOU WILL ALSO NEED YOUR KEYBOARD.

During the video section

The first time you are asked to stop the tape you should familiarize yourself with the layout of your keyboard. Find middle C, and then locate all the other Cs.

The second time you are asked to stop the tape you should play the five-finger exercise with your right hand, beginning on middle C.

The third time you are asked to stop the tape you should play the chord using your thumb, middle finger and little finger (that is, fingers 1, 3 and 5).

The fourth time you are asked to stop the tape you should play the five-finger exercise starting on middle C with your left hand. Then play the chord.

After the video section

I hope that you are now beginning to feel comfortable when playing your keyboard. The five-finger exercises and the chord you have been playing form the first stages in learning how to manipulate your fingers independently. Another stage, in which this skill is developed further, will follow in Unit 3.

Summary

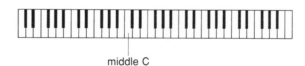

middle C

Figure 14   Location of middle C on a five-octave keyboard. Your keyboard may have a wider range.

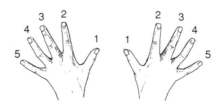

Figure 15   Numbering convention for fingering.

10 SOME PRACTICAL WORK (II)

10.1 THE OCTAVE

During the video section you found middle C on your keyboard. Do this again now, playing it with the index finger of your left hand.

  PLAY.

Now, release the note. Then, find the next C up the keyboard and play that with the index finger of your right hand. Release the note. Now play both notes together, middle C and the higher C. Hold the notes down while you listen carefully to the composite sound. Release.

That sound is the sound of an **octave**, the most fundamental interval in music. It is fundamental to Western musicians and to the vast majority of non-Western musicians, and thus is virtually universal. The two notes that comprise the octave sound almost alike, yet one is in a different **register** from another: the upper note is in a higher register than the lower one.

Acoustically the interval of the octave has the simplest ratio between the frequencies of its two pitches of any interval. For example, we know that the note A used for tuning an orchestra usually has the frequency 440 hertz. The A an octave higher has the frequency 880 hertz. The frequency ratio of the upper A to the lower one is 2:1. And this ratio can also be observed in the length of the string or pipe used to produce the sound. For instance, if a stretched string is made to vibrate, the pitch, produced by 'stopping' the string at its mid-point, and thus dividing it into two equal segments, will be an octave higher than that produced by the whole string vibrating (see Figure 16).

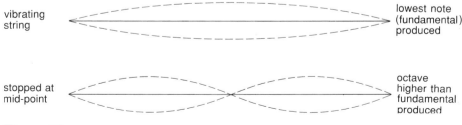

Figure 16

The ratio of the segments to the whole is 2:1 and the discovery of this relationship is attributed to the Greek mathematician and religious teacher Pythagoras. He also worked out ratios for several other intervals, but these ratios are more complex. Thus the octave, the most fundamental interval, has the simplest ratio.

Exercise 12

Let us now listen to several different intervals, some of which will be octaves. Remind yourself of the sound you are listening for by playing the two Cs on your keyboard again. Then listen to audio-cassette Item 20, which contains ten pairs of successive notes, and write down which are octaves and which are not. Answers can be found at the back of the unit.

  LISTEN NOW TO ITEM 20.

Discussion

If you had difficulty with that exercise, remember that with an octave you are listening for what sounds like the same note, but is in a different register. Alternatively, you can use a well-known tune as a yardstick with which to test the interval. An obvious one that springs to mind is the song *Somewhere Over the Rainbow*. The two syllables of 'Some-where' are set to a rising octave. If you had some incorrect answers, try and sing or hum 'Some-where' to fit each of the pairs of notes in turn. This could help.

Since we have moved on to real music, we shall follow our exercise using octaves in the abstract, as you might say, with some octaves from real music.

Exercise 13

On audio-cassette Item 21, you will hear ten short extracts of music, some of which begin with octaves, some of which do not. Which is which? You may have to listen several times to the extracts because not all are in a conveniently slow tempo – in fact they are mostly in a medium tempo and one is quite fast. In addition, you will have to be very quick off the mark with extracts (d) and (j)! So be prepared to listen several times before you give your answer. You will have to become familiar with each extract before you can make your choice of whether there is an octave or not. Incidentally, all the octaves are rising, except one. Answers can be found at the back of the unit.

 LISTEN NOW TO ITEM 21.

Discussion

The extracts that might have proved a problem were (f) and (h), which have wide intervals, but not as wide as an octave, and (i) which was so fast that you might have had trouble focusing on the opening interval. However, if you had incorrect answers for any of the extracts, listen again.

CHECKPOINT

You have now had some practice at recognizing aurally the interval of an octave (see Section 5, second aim).

10.2 SCALES

Play middle C once again with your left hand and the higher C with your right.

 PLAY.

We have seen that this is an octave, but what happens in between? What about the other notes on the keyboard – the pitches that come in between the two Cs? As you can see from your keyboard, the physical distance between the one C and the other, quite a large step, is filled in with smaller steps. In fact, if you count middle C as number one, you can count eight white notes to reach the higher C. This gives seven steps between the Cs. Play those eight notes using whatever fingers are convenient and listen to these small steps.

 PLAY.

That is one way of dividing up the octave: with eight notes (hence the name, octave) and seven steps. Now play not only the white notes between the two Cs, but the black ones as well. As before, use whichever fingers are con-

venient and count middle C as number one. This time, there are thirteen notes and twelve small steps.

 PLAY.

This division of the octave into a series of small steps creates **scales**, and you have already played two different ones. But it does not take much imagination to realize that even with the notes available on your keyboard a considerable number of scales is possible by simply using a selection of these notes. For instance, you might have a scale that starts on middle C and has the notes shown by crosses in Figure 17.

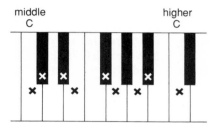

Figure 17

Once again, try playing this scale on your keyboard using the most convenient fingering.

If you now listen to audio-cassette Item 22, you will hear an extract from a piece of music based on this scale (although you won't hear the scale played as such). It comes from the opening of the last movement of *Quatuor pour la fin du temps* (*Quartet for the End of Time*) composed by Olivier Messiaen in 1940.

 LISTEN NOW TO ITEM 22.

The particular notes chosen for the scale obviously help to dictate the distinctive sound-world that is produced when music is composed using the scale.

But are we restricted to using only those pitches found on the keyboard? You can answer this question yourself by trying the following experiment, which is in two parts. First of all, take a deep breath and, starting at middle C, sing a continuous note gradually getting higher and higher in pitch until you reach the octave C. By the way, this type of continuously rising (or falling) pitch is called a **glissando**.

SING.

Now, for the second part. Take an even deeper breath, and sing up from middle C to the higher C again, but this time stop each time you have produced a different pitch. How many different pitches are there?

SING.

There are as many pitches as your ear can differentiate!

If you could distinguish each frequency rise of 1 Hz between middle C (261.63 Hz) and the upper C (523.25 Hz), then you could hear over 250 different pitches! But the ear/brain mechanism for distinguishing these pitches is not as sensitive as this, and the smallest audible change in pitch

Figure 18   Olivier Messiaen (1908–1992), about 1938. French composer, teacher and ornithologist. Several of his compositions use ideas derived from birdsong. (Photo: Studio Harcourt)

within this particular frequency band (i.e. roughly 260–520 Hz) consists of several Hz. The perception of the smallest audible change in pitch, as with the upper and lower limits of audibility, varies from person to person and the discriminatory power of the ear can be improved with practice. However, there is very little correlation between having a high discriminatory power and being a professional musician rather than a member of the general public. On the other hand, among performing musicians, those who have to tune their instrument develop a greater discriminatory power than those who do not (as one would imagine).

10.3 HOLDING ON

Discriminating between different pitches is clearly of primary importance for musicians. Another useful skill is to be able to hold on to specific pitches, either by singing them while other notes are being sounded, or by holding them in the head as a sort of anchor point whilst other pitches are sounded. Let us consider the former skill first.

As the course progresses and you are asked to write successions of chords (that is, two or more notes sounded simultaneously), you will come to realize that with music composed during the period covered by the course, the lowest line of notes, the 'bass line', is very important. Of course, the most important line in the music will be the tune or melody and this will normally be in the top part. However, the lowest part forms the basis for the harmony and as such will become a focal point, either in theory so to speak as you write down your bass lines, or in practice as you try to *hear* them whilst writing them.

Unfortunately, if you have never tried to concentrate on anything but the top part of a piece of music before, listening for lower parts is by no means easy. It is a skill that has to be practised and, indeed takes a considerable time to develop – months, I'm afraid, rather than weeks or days! Nevertheless it is worth cultivating, even at the basic level we shall be attempting here, because it makes one aware that music usually consists of not only melodies, but also what can broadly be called accompaniment. (The exception, where there is just a single line of unaccompanied melody, is called **monody**.) As we write harmonies we shall want to hear not only the top part but the other parts as well. So let us start by attempting two basic exercises.

You have already listened to series of paired pitches in order to discover the higher of two notes and to identify octaves. If you listen to audio-cassette Item 23, you will hear another series of pitches in pairs, five in all. Each pair will begin with the lower pitch and this will be held for a little while. Join in, singing that pitch out loud while it is sustained. Then a higher pitch will join the lower one. Continue singing the lower pitch. Finally the lower pitch will disappear but the upper one will remain. Continue singing the lower one. Take breaths when you run out!

 LISTEN AND SING: ITEM 23.

Could you keep the lower pitch going? If not, then try again!

You might have found it difficult to sing the lower note of each pair; you couldn't locate the given pitch. If so, try first of all to find the lower note on your keyboard. Decide whether it is located roughly in the middle of the keyboard or to the right or left by trying to match the note with ones on the keyboard. Then narrow your focus to the relevant area of the keyboard playing several more notes to find the exact match. Once you have found the correct note concentrate on it as hard as possible, either humming it in your head or out loud. When you have succeeded with this, return once more to the audio-cassette and try the exercise again, humming the lower note in your head if you prefer.

Now, a somewhat more advanced exercise. On audio-cassette Item 24, there are another five pairs of pitches. This time, however, they are sounded simultaneously. You have to sing the lower pitch, either in your head, or out loud. After each pair, there will be a short break, and then the lower pitch is sounded by itself – in other words the correct answer! See how you get on.

 LISTEN AND SING: ITEM 24.

Perhaps you sing in a choir and regularly sing one of the lower parts, such as the alto part (women with low singing voices or men with very high singing voices), or the tenor part (men with high singing voices), or the bass part (men with low singing voices). If you do, you will have had plenty of experience of focusing on pitches other than those sung by the sopranos (women with high singing voices). But if you have not had this type of experience, turning your attention away from the top part to a low one is difficult. But do persevere. A strong mental effort is needed, but as ever, repeated practice should produce an improvement.

CHECKPOINT

The aim of the last two exercises was to help you towards identifying the lower of two notes sounding together (see Section 5, third aim).

Exercise 14

Finally, for our last exercise in this unit, here is another variant of holding on to pitches. Instead of trying to concentrate on one of two pitches sounding simultaneously, we are now going to hold on to a pitch in our memory while others intervene. Much Western music is built on a principle analogous to taking a journey: you set out from home, enjoy several temporary resting places en route, and finally return home. Therefore retaining a memory of home is necessary if you want to compare it with the intervening resting places. For our purposes here, 'home' is going to be a certain pitch, and we are going to undertake a journey via other pitches, but try to retain the memory of the home pitch. If you listen to audio-cassette Item 25, you will hear seven series of pitches and each series will be repeated twice. All the series will start out from the same pitch, the home pitch. Some time during each series there will be a return to the home pitch, but only once, and not necessarily for the last note of the series. You have to spot which is the repetition of the home pitch. In the boxes in Figure 19, place a tick for the second home pitch (ticks for the first home pitch have already been entered in the first box of each row). The first row is completed for you. Answers can be found at the back of the unit.

1 ☑ ☐ ☐ ☑

2 ☑ ☐ ☐ ☐

3 ☑ ☐ ☐ ☐ ☐

4 ☑ ☐ ☐ ☐ ☐

5 ☑ ☐ ☐ ☐ ☐ ☐

6 ☑ ☐ ☐ ☐ ☐ ☐ ☐

7 ☑ ☐ ☐ ☐ ☐ ☐ ☐ ☐

Figure 19

 LISTEN NOW TO ITEM 25.

A musical memory is obviously an essential requisite for a musician, whether composer, performer or listener. Music exists in time and therefore without a musical memory the listener simply would not make sense of the music. And indeed the vast majority of listeners have a fairly well-developed musical memory; most people can remember tunes and take pleasure in whistling, humming or singing them. The series of pitches you have just been listening to are really like simple short tunes – although not very distinctive ones as they lack rhythmic interest – and they are fairly straightforward to remember. But imagine trying to remember pieces of music on a much larger scale – movements from symphonies, sections of operas, and so on – and not only the tune but the rest of the texture too. It is possible to do this with enough time and mental application, and moreover it is essential for a pianist giving a recital or a conductor conducting from memory. Every detail has to be known. But even for the ordinary listener, the pleasure of listening to music can be enhanced by remembering roughly where certain events happen in a large-scale piece, where certain tunes are repeated, where certain rhythms appear, and so on. If you can recognize the relationship of different elements in a piece to others, and form a mental picture of the shape of the music, this too is a bonus. Thus developing one's musical memory is an important task for the musician and the previous exercise is one step along that path. Try listening again if you had difficulty, concentrating as hard as possible on the home pitch. As a last resort, it might help to hum the home pitch continuously throughout each extract, noting whether the other pitches coincide or not. But you will have to concentrate hard!

11 SUMMARY

In the second part of this unit where we have concentrated on pitch, you have been introduced to certain musical concepts and terms, as well as particular skills, and it is advisable that you master these before going on to Unit 3. Therefore when reading the list below, try and be as honest with yourself as possible about your success at coping with these new concepts and skills, and if you feel unhappy with your progress with any of them refer back to the relevant sections. So, before proceeding to Unit 3, ask yourself whether you can:

1   recognize the difference between indefinite and definite pitches (Section 6.1);

2   provide a definition of pitch (Section 6.3);

3   distinguish between the higher and lower notes of two pitches sounding successively (Section 7);

4   locate middle C on your keyboard (video);

5   play reasonably fluently with either hand a five-finger exercise and a three-note chord (video);

6   distinguish the interval of an octave from other intervals (Section 10.1);

7   sing the lower of two pitches sounding simultaneously (Section 10.3);

8   hold a particular pitch in your memory while others intervene (Section 10.3).

12 MORE AURAL TRAINING

Finally this week, here are some more aural tests. These are similar to the tests in Section 4 but increase the difficulty in two ways: firstly, by including some more complex rhythms, and secondly, by introducing notes of two different pitches. These tests will therefore consolidate and extend your ability to identify and notate rhythmic patterns, and at the same time will enable you to assess your ability to discriminate between different pitches.

Each test will contain only two different pitches. To notate these, you will need manuscript paper containing five-line staves. I suggest you place the higher notes on the top line of the stave and the lower notes on the bottom line, like this:

You will find the tests on audio-cassette Item 26. The procedure followed is the same as in Section 4. You will hear:

1   An announcement of the test number.

2   An announcement of the time signature for the test.

3   Some introductory beats to give you the tempo.

4   The test itself (which again will begin on the first beat of a bar).

5   The introductory beats and the test again.

6   The announcement 'now check your answer against that in the unit'.

The answers are at the back of this unit (p. 47).

If you need to, look back at Section 4 for advice on method. Of course, if you're using any kind of shorthand, you will have to indicate to yourself the different pitches as well as the rhythmic outline.

A reasonable performance on these tests implies that you're doing very well on the course so far. After all, you have been studying for only two weeks! If you're struggling a bit, don't despair. Training the ear takes time. Try to come back to these tests sometime during the next two or three weeks and have another attempt.

 NOW TRY THE AURAL TESTS IN ITEM 26.

ANSWERS TO EXERCISES

EXERCISE 10

Each answer describes the pitch of the first note relative to the second.

1	Higher	6	Higher
2	Higher	7	Lower
3	Lower	8	Same
4	Same	9	Lower
5	Lower	10	Higher

EXERCISE 11

Each answer describes the pitch of the first note relative to the second.

1	Lower	6	Higher
2	Higher	7	Higher
3	Same	8	Lower
4	Lower	9	Higher
5	Same	10	Lower

EXERCISE 12

1	Octave	6	Not an octave
2	Not an octave	7	Octave
3	Not an octave	8	Not an octave
4	Octave	9	Octave
5	Octave	10	Octave

EXERCISE 13

(a)	Octave	(f)	Not an octave
(b)	Not an octave	(g)	Octave (falling)
(c)	Not an octave	(h)	Not an octave
(d)	Octave	(i)	Octave
(e)	Octave	(j)	Octave

EXERCISE 14

See Figure 20.

1 ☑ ☐ ☐ ☑
2 ☑ ☐ ☑ ☐
3 ☑ ☐ ☐ ☐ ☑
4 ☑ ☐ ☑ ☐ ☐
5 ☑ ☐ ☐ ☑ ☐ ☐
6 ☑ ☐ ☐ ☐ ☐ ☑ ☐
7 ☑ ☐ ☐ ☐ ☐ ☐ ☐ ☑

Figure 20

ANSWERS TO AURAL TESTS IN SECTION 4

Aural Test 1

Aural Test 2

Aural Test 3

Aural Test 4

Aural Test 5

Aural Test 6

Aural Test 7

Aural Test 8

Aural Test 9

Aural Test 10

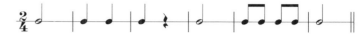

Aural Test 11

Aural Test 12

ANSWERS TO AURAL TESTS IN SECTION 12

Aural Test 13

Aural Test 14

Aural Test 15

Aural Test 16

Aural Test 17

Aural Test 18

Aural Test 19

Aural Test 20

ACKNOWLEDGEMENTS

Figure 1   Reproduced by permission of Editio Musica, Budapest.

Figures 7 and 10(a)   Boosey and Hawkes Ltd.

Figure 18   Bibliothèque Nationale, Paris.

The Course Team also wishes to thank the Royal College of Music, and the following for their participation in the video material: Julia Stewart (violin), Paul Saunders (clarinet) and Charlie Dochertie (horn).

UNIT 3

STARTING WITH STAFF NOTATION

Prepared for the Course Team by Trevor Bray

CONTENTS

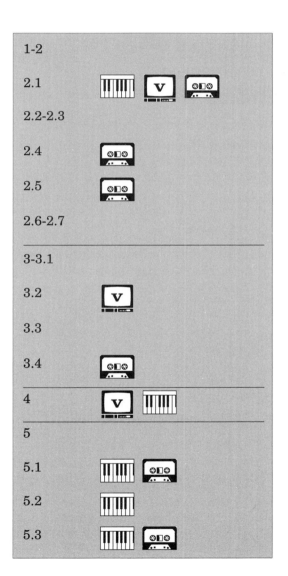

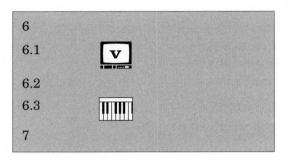

All audio items for this unit are on Audio-cassette 2.

All video items for this unit are on Video-cassette 1.

1   CONTENT AND AIMS

Your introduction to the basic elements of music has concentrated on rhythm and pitch. These different elements have been separated for ease of learning, but in reality they are interdependent. In this unit, they are combined as we progress to a study of staff notation. This type of music notation, which uses mainly graphic means to represent sounds, began in the West during the ninth century, and despite being developed considerably has remained the most important system for notating music in the West to this day.

At first, staff notation will be introduced through its constituent elements, and to a certain extent these elements will be placed within a historical context. Do not try to remember all the details of this contextual material; it has been introduced only so that you will understand why certain features of staff notation have evolved in the form they have. The main bulk of the teaching will, in fact, be carried out through practical activities, and hence two main sections of the unit, Sections 3 and 6, have been reserved for writing out short music examples using the treble and bass clefs. Frequent practice of both the writing and playing of the examples should make you familiar with the way staff notation works and increase your fluency in reading it.

2   THE ELEMENTS OF STAFF NOTATION

2.1   EQUIVALENCE

One piece of music you can be said to have 'learned' already is shown in Example 1. It consists of a combination of the two exercises we practised during Video Section 1 in Unit 2 – the 'five-finger' exercise and the 'chord' exercise – and written down in staff notation it looks like this:

Example 1

This introduces a considerable number of new notational concepts that I'll be explaining later during the unit. But even now you may well be able to

51

'follow' the music for yourself. If you need to, run through the video section again, playing the two exercises once more, and then try to play the combined version of the exercises given as Example 1. Remember that on the video we began with the thumb of our right hand placed on middle C, and that the three-note chord (which comes at the end of the example) was played by depressing the thumb, middle and small fingers simultaneously. Remember too, from Unit 1, that a minim (♩) has two beats, whereas a crotchet (♩) has only one. If you bear these points in mind while following the fingering suggested for each note you should be able to play Example 1. Try now, but don't hurry!

 PLAY.

In order to check that you have played Example 1 correctly, listen to audio-cassette Item 1, and compare the sound there with what you produced.

 LISTEN NOW TO ITEM 1.

While playing Example 1, you were not absorbing every detail of the information supplied, since, as I suggested, some of these details have not been explained as yet. Nevertheless, even without explanation, certain features of the notation provide some clues as to what should be happening. For instance, for the first five notes of Example 1, the note-heads are placed higher and higher on the grid of horizontal lines so that as the pitches rise higher and higher so do their visual counterparts, the note-heads. Similarly, the note-heads for notes 6–9 appear visually to get lower and lower as do those pitches. In addition, the final three notes, which are played simultaneously as a chord, are aligned vertically and thus contrast with the other notes. These other notes are spaced out in a linear fashion which suggests that they should be played successively rather than simultaneously, or at least played in a different manner than the last three notes. Thus, simply from the appearance of staff notation on the page we can deduce two very important facts about it:

1 that the *note-heads* mark the pitch;
2 that notes sounding simultaneously are aligned vertically, whereas notes that follow each other are arranged linearly.

In a music notation such equivalence between what you hear and what you see is clearly helpful, and examples of this equivalence have existed in the notation of West European music for a long time. Figure 1 contains one of the earliest examples of West European music notations, dating from the ninth century, and you can see a succession of signs placed above the written text of the left-hand column. These signs, called **neumes**, although not situated on horizontal lines that could indicate pitch exactly, suggest a contour of pitches (grouped around an imaginary line) and could well jog a confused or failing memory into remembering the correct notes. Indeed, neumes were added to the less well-known melodies; others, because well-known and easily memorable, did not need such treatment.

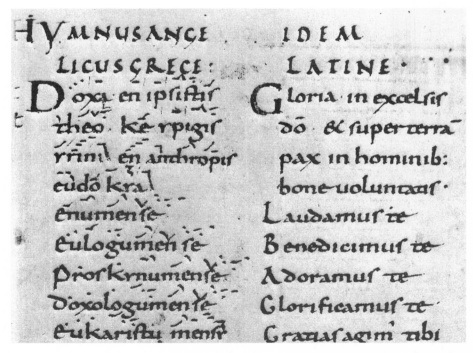

Figure 1   A ninth-century manuscript showing neumes (written above the lines of the left-hand text). The parallel Greek and Latin texts are taken from the Gloria of the Mass.

Even without being able to appreciate all the details involved with the notation of Example 1, then, we can gain some help from it. But what do we need to know to gain the most benefit from it?

2.2 FROM LEFT TO RIGHT

One characteristic of staff notation is that we read it from left to right. This point might seem too obvious to mention, and indeed we took it for granted when we 'read' Example 1. Yet, interestingly, this is not the case for all music notations. In any given culture, the path traced by the notation across the page usually follows that used for writing script in that culture. Therefore where the script is written from the top to the bottom of the page, and starting at the top right-hand corner, as in China, Korea and (to a certain extent) Japan, the music notations trace a similar path. In Western Europe, the system of writing from left to right and top to bottom has led to staff notation being written so that it follows the same path. Thus time is represented by a horizontal axis.

2.3 THE STAVE (OR STAFF) AND NOTE-HEADS

The idea of placing note-heads on a set of horizontal lines – the staff or stave – to show explicitly the relationship of various pitches with each other emerged in Western music towards the end of the ninth century. In the ninth-century music treatise, *Musica enchiriadis*, an eight-line staff is used (Figure 2).

Figure 2   Lines forming a staff in the ninth-century treatise Musica enchiriadis.

Later, the music theorist, Guido of Arezzo, while not proposing a standard number of lines for the stave, did suggest, in his *Aliae regulae* (*c.* 1030), that lines should be drawn for every other pitch, so that alternate pitches sat *on* the lines and the remaining pitches were placed in the intervening spaces *between* the lines. This principle was adopted subsequently. By the thirteenth century, it became apparent that the five-line stave, in combination with Guido's principle, was ideal for the notation of the vocal lines then being written (see Figure 3); the range of notes used fitted conveniently on this type of stave.

Figure 3   Four- and five-line staves from a thirteenth-century manuscript. The stave lines have faded, but the black dots on the right show their positions.

For the past 300 years the five-line stave has become the norm too. However, before that, when coping with wider ranges, more lines were added to the stave from time to time; for example, for fourteenth-century Italian vocal music, where a six-line stave was adopted (Figure 4).

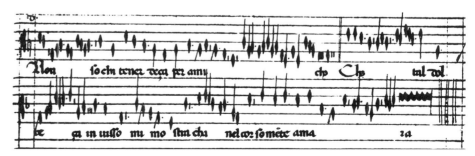

Figure 4   Six-line staves used for fourteenth-century Italian vocal music.

The wider range of notes needed in keyboard music led to staves with even more lines. Figure 5 shows the eight-line stave used by Adam Ileborgh in his tablature[1] of 1448 for the right-hand part (the left-hand part is written below the stave using an alphabetic notation).

Figure 5   An eight-line stave used for the right-hand part of a fifteenth-century keyboard piece (possibly composed for the organ).

Occasionally the music for both hands was notated on the same stave (Figure 6). With such a large array of lines, however, the visual effect becomes confusing and two staves of five lines each, one for the right hand and one for the left, became the norm. In fact, staves of more than five lines were rarely used after the seventeenth century.

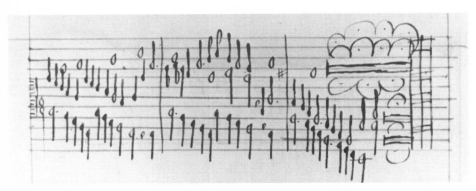

Figure 6   A twelve-line stave, taken from The Mulliner Book (c. 1550–75), a collection of keyboard pieces.

[1]   Although tablatures use some of the graphic signs found in staff notation, they use primarily letters or numbers to notate music.

Not only do Figures 3–6 show different sizes of the stave, they also illustrate a diversity of shapes for the note-heads; square, rectangular, lozenge-shaped and round. Some note-heads are filled in; some left void. From time to time, additional colours were used. For instance, where black was the main colour, red, or red and blue might have been used to designate yet further different rhythmic values. The scholar intent on transcribing these older notations into modern notation must learn the rhythmic relationships suggested by the different note-heads (and, additionally, the note-stems where present). Conversely, a detailed knowledge of the various shapes of the note-heads and stems can be used by a scholar to date a manuscript being transcribed. But for our purposes, suffice it to say that although the lozenge-shaped notes typical of the fourteenth century (see Figure 4) continued to be used until the sixteenth century, already during the fifteenth century rounded shapes began to appear and in time became the norm. No plausible explanation has been suggested to account for this change in shape!

2.4   CLEFS

The use of the stave together with note-heads for individual pitches, as in Example 2, can supply us with information about the relationship of the pitches with each other.

Example 2

Yet, as it stands, the first note in Example 2 could be any pitch we care to choose. If we wish to specify a particular pitch or series of pitches we need some sort of guide: a sign that will enable us to indicate the pitch. That sign is supplied by a clef (from the Latin, *clavis*, meaning 'key'; the French for 'key' is in fact *clef*). The first use of a sign to indicate the specific pitch of a note on the stave comes in the *Musica enchiriadis* (see Figure 2, the column of signs to the right of the column of letters TSTTT etc.). By the eleventh century, roman letters were adopted. In Figure 3, examples of these can be seen clearly at the beginning of the stave. They are the letters g, c and f. Indeed these three letters, in stylized forms, became the norm for the three different types of clef used in staff notation. Thus, in a stylized form, the letter g is now used as the treble clef. Its rather flamboyant stylization, with its curls and flourishes, designates that the second line from the bottom is G. Notice how the clef is drawn so that it begins on the second line from the bottom and how it then proceeds to circle around this line. It also tells us that this G is the one *above* middle C.

Example 3

G

This sign, the clef, is of vital importance, because it opens up all sorts of possibilities. For instance, you know the whereabouts of middle C on your keyboard and you now know by referring to Example 1 that you played the note G with the little finger of your right hand. Therefore you can now play Example 4.

Example 4

First of all, try playing this without any fingering given.

 PLAY.

Exercise

If you weren't successful, consider the fingering in Example 1 and then add the relevant fingering to Example 4, writing it above the stave.

Answer

The fingering should be as in Example 5.

Example 5

Now, try playing the example again.

 PLAY.

Designating the note G with the treble clef permits us to add names to all the pitches we have been using so far. With C for the lowest pitch and G for the highest, we can fill in the other letters from the alphabet.

Example 6

C D E F G

Before proceeding, memorize the letter names for these notes. We shall return to them later.

? PAUSE.

Notice several important points here. First, for the letter-names of notes, you proceed forward through the alphabet as the pitch rises and backwards as the pitch falls. Secondly, the letters come from the opening of the alphabet. Only seven letters are used, A–G, and when G is reached, you return to A. Finally, middle C is special in that it sits on its own line, which has to be drawn in for each occurrence of the note. This is called a **leger** (or **ledger**) **line**; leger lines may be found both below and above the stave. They simply represent further lines of the stave, but since the five-line stave has become the norm, are added only when needed. Incidentally, although middle C has a leger line, D does not.

Example 7

 not

Placing the treble clef on the stave so that it begins on the second line from the bottom has become the norm because the ranges of soprano and alto parts then sit conveniently on the stave, as does much writing for such instruments as the violin, flute and oboe. In theory, there is no reason why the treble clef cannot be moved so that it starts on any other line, but in practice its only other position has been on the bottom line. Of course, if we move the treble clef from the second line from the bottom to the bottom line itself, the note that we have learned as E in Example 6 now becomes G. And C becomes E, D becomes F, and so on. (But do not bother to memorize these 'new' notes. You will not be asked to use anything other than the 'normal' treble clef on this course!) This position was favoured by the French during the seventeenth and eighteenth centuries for violin or flute/recorder parts or, in vocal music, for the soprano part. You can hear the effect of moving the clef by listening to audio-cassette Item 2. First you will hear Example 4 (and you can therefore check that you were playing this correctly) and then Example 8, which has the same pattern of note-heads but with the treble clef moved from the second line to the bottom line.

Example 8   Note names with the treble clef on the bottom line

 LISTEN NOW TO ITEM 2, FOLLOWING EXAMPLES 4 AND 8.

If we replace the treble clef by either the bass clef (the F clef) or the C clef, the aural difference is even more striking. Listen to audio-cassette Item 3, following Example 9.

Example 9

 LISTEN NOW TO ITEM 3 AND FOLLOW EXAMPLE 9.

The bass (or F) clef is currently used for the lower-sounding instruments, bass voices and for the left hand of keyboard instruments, and as the course progresses you will become thoroughly familiar with its usage. As yet you

Figure 7   An oboe. It has a double reed, and is a member of the woodwind family.

Figure 8   A recorder. Recorders exist in a range of sizes; this is a treble recorder.

Figure 9   A flute. One of the woodwind instruments, though modern instruments are made of metal.

need not worry about the names of the notes in the example above, but suffice it to say that the bass clef shows the whereabouts of the note F *below* middle C and that the clef is drawn so that it begins on that note. In Example 9 the bass clef is placed on the second line from the top of the stave, its standard position. You will also need to become familiar with the C clef since the music for several orchestral instruments is notated using this clef. Both the F and C clefs can be moved up and down the stave so that they mark other lines for F and C respectively. The C clef can be placed on each of the five lines, but in modern usage only the following positions of the C clef appear:

Example 10

Middle C ⟶ 𝄡 for the viola

Middle C ⟶ 𝄡 for the higher notes of the cello, bassoon and trombone

The first is known as the **alto clef** and the second as the **tenor clef**, and you will be introduced to the C clef in more detail when you come to Unit 14.

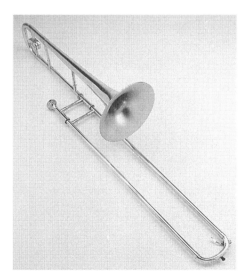

Figure 10   A trombone. A brass instrument with a moveable slide, enabling different sets of notes to be played.

Figure 11   A bassoon. A woodwind instrument with a double reed.

Incidentally, both the F and C clefs, like the G clef, are (as I mentioned previously) stylizations of roman letters, unlikely though that might appear. In Figure 3, you saw that the Roman letters C and F are clearly visible to the left of the staves. However, these soon became stylized. On a late fourteenth-century manuscript (Figure 12a) you see both a stylized C clef sitting astride the second line of the stave from the top and a stylized F clef astride the fourth line down. Figure 12(b) compares the stylized letters to their modern counterparts.

Figure 12(a)   A late fourteenth-century manuscript showing C and F clefs.

▮ = C and ◆▮ = F

Figure 12(b)   Stylized letters used as clefs in Figure 12(a).

The current shape of these clefs relates somewhat more readily (but not entirely!) to these fourteenth-century examples than the original roman letters.

CHECKPOINT

> **Clefs** are placed at the beginning of staves to denote the pitch of a particular line and therefore the pitches of the other lines together with the spaces in between the lines. Three clefs are in current usage, the **treble clef** indicating the note G above middle C, the **bass clef** indicating the note F below middle C and the **C clef** indicating middle C itself.

2.5   THE TIME SIGNATURE

The time signature that comes at the beginning of our original example, Example 1, together with the note values present, have already been explained in Unit 1. Hence, when you first played Example 1, the rhythm should have caused you no problem! The following two examples should not be too difficult for you to play either. Although they use two other time signatures and a larger number of rhythmic durations, the pattern of the pitches is roughly the same as in Example 1. The first is in ¾.

Example 11

You might feel more secure if you write in the fingering, and it will also help if you count along with the music in order to play the quavers in the correct time. Subdivide each beat into two by counting 'ONE-and-two-and-three-and-ONE-and-two etc.'. If you tap out the rhythm first, before you play the notes, this could also give you more confidence.

 TAP AND COUNT THE RHYTHM, THEN PLAY.

The correct version can be heard on the audio-cassette as Item 4.

 LISTEN NOW TO ITEM 4.

Practise this until you can play it correctly. Notice the use of the dot in bar 3, which lengthens the rhythmic value of the C by half as much again. Also there is less time here to prepare yourself for playing the three-note chord, but it has to come spot on the first beat of bar 4!

During Unit 2, you were also introduced to compound time (Section 3), and so here is an example using the time signature ⁶⁄₈.

Example 12

Notice here that the main beat is a dotted crotchet. This is because the example has a compound time signature and the dotted crotchet is subdivided into three quavers (which add up to a dotted crotchet). Thus since there are six quavers per bar, it is easier at this stage to count in quavers rather than in dotted crotchet beats. Try playing the example now, a little more slowly than you played Example 11. Tap out the rhythm first if this helps.

 TAP AND COUNT THE RHYTHM, THEN PLAY.

Listen to Item 5 on the audio-cassette for the correct version.

 LISTEN NOW TO ITEM 5.

2.6 DYNAMIC MARKINGS

An important feature of staff notation was absent from Example 1. There were no markings for dynamics. These are used to signify the variations of loudness and softness in the music, and the most common are **piano** (meaning 'soft'), and **forte** (meaning 'loud'), together with **pianissimo** (very soft), and **fortissimo** (very loud). Often these terms are abbreviated, and a useful range of volume-levels can be distinguished when using these and related markings. See Table 1.

Table 1 Dynamic markings

ppp	
pp	pianissimo
p	piano
mp	mezzo piano (literally 'half softly')
mf	mezzo forte (literally 'half loudly')
f	forte
ff	fortissimo
fff	

Notice that the terms used are Italian. When dynamic marks began to appear during the seventeenth century, such was the dominance of Italian music (or, rather, Italian *printed* music) that many Italian words were adopted by musicians, including not only these dynamic markings, but also those for tempo markings (see below) and many others, e.g. cantata, concerto, opera, sonata, and so on.

The more pronounced use of dynamic contrast during the seventeenth century and into the first half of the eighteenth, and the ever more variable dynamic level of music composed during the following 150 years, led composers to include dynamic markings more and more frequently until by the early twentieth century some composers included a welter of dynamic markings in their scores. For instance, if you glance through your score of Corelli's Concerto Grosso, Op. 6, No. 4 (published 1714, and reproduced in *Scores 1*), you will see that there are few dynamic markings – and then only *p*[*iano*] and *f*[*orte*]. Compare that with the final five bars of Grainger's piano arrangement of his own *Colonial Song* (1911), where there are many more dynamic markings per bar and which uses a greater variety, ranging from *ppp* to *fff*.

Example 13   Grainger, Colonial Song

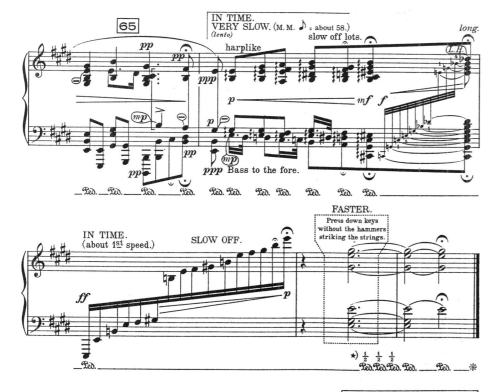

In the Grainger example, you can see another means of indicating changes in loudness, this time by graphic means rather than words or letters:

 ◁ means 'becoming gradually louder'

 ▷ means 'becoming gradually softer'.

Words, frequently abbreviated, are also used to indicate the same effects: **crescendo** (**cresc.**) for becoming louder and **decrescendo** (**decresc.**) or **diminuendo** (**dim.**) for getting softer. Another dynamic marking commonly found is **sf** or **sfz**. These are abbreviations of **sforzando**, which indicates a sudden brief burst of loudness, accentuating a note. As with all the terms mentioned above, this comes from Italian, and means 'forced' or 'compelling'.

Of course, these dynamic markings do not suggest an absolute series of volume levels. They are used to suggest relative levels of volume, and the particular levels heard during a performance will depend on many variable circumstances: the size of the hall in which the performance takes place, the instrument being played, the musicality of the performer, and so on. Dynamic markings are a guide, and are to be interpreted by the performer (although in Example 13 Grainger does not give the performer much room to manoeuvre). A further point to mention is that an absence of dynamic markings does not mean that the music should be played at entirely one level of volume. For instance, to suggest that because music written before the seventeenth century is devoid of dynamic markings it should be performed at one volume-level is ridiculous. Even in the Corelli concerto, during passages provided *with* a dynamic marking, the volume-level will vary almost from note to note as the player 'shapes' the music. It is in fact difficult to sustain a given level of volume for even a short period when playing most instruments, and for budding performers just as much time has to be spent learning how to sustain a volume-level as to vary it.

2.7   TEMPO MARKINGS

One final feature of staff notation needs to be mentioned, and you have been making use of it already. It is the tempo marking, which is placed at the start of a piece above the stave. Tempo markings, like dynamic markings, began to be used in significant numbers during the seventeenth century. As with dynamics they are usually drawn from Italian, despite the occasional use of corresponding terms from other languages, particularly during the nineteenth and early twentieth centuries. These Italian terms, then, have for all intents and purposes become the *lingua franca* for tempo markings and you therefore need to become conversant with their meanings. Some of those most commonly met are listed in Table 2.

Table 2   Tempo markings

Tempo mark	Translation	Interpretation
Largo	large, broad	Very slowly
Adagio	at ease, leisurely	Slowly, or very slowly
Andante	at a walking pace	At a walking pace
Moderato	moderate, restrained	Moderately
Vivace	flourishing, full of life	Lively
Allegro	merry, cheerful	Fast
Presto	ready, prompt	Very fast (although originally only fast)

Once again, these tempo markings are not absolute. Each does not denote one tempo and only one. Tempo markings are, rather, guides to the performer and moreover have been interpreted differently at different times. For example, an Adagio movement composed by Corelli during the late seventeenth century will probably be played at a faster tempo than an Adagio movement written by Beethoven during the early nineteenth century. On the other hand, both will be played in a *relatively* slow tempo, not a fast one.

Occasionally composers like to vary the tempo of a piece as it proceeds, and three useful terms here, yet again drawn from Italian, are **accelerando** (**accel**.), becoming quicker, and the reverse, **rallentando** (**rall**.), or, for a more localized slowing down, **ritenuto** (**rit**.), which literally means 'held back'. As you proceed through the course you will come across these terms pretty frequently.

CHECKPOINT

This introduction to staff notation has included of necessity much information, and you may well be suffering from mental indigestion at the moment! However, during subsequent sections of this unit we shall be consolidating material learnt in this section by writing down some notes on paper using both the treble and bass clefs. Meanwhile, the main points that you need to retain from this section are:

1   the position of the treble clef on the stave;
2   the letter-names of the five notes we have learnt while using the treble clef;
3   the Italian terms we have met and what they indicate.

Make sure that you are conversant with these points before you continue any further.

Figure 13(a)   Manuscript of Beethoven's Cello Sonata, Op. 102, No. 1.

Figure 13(b)   Manuscript of Bach's Partita No. 3 for solo violin.

Figure 13(c)   Manuscript of Stravinsky's The Rite of Spring.

3 NOTES ON PAPER I: THE TREBLE CLEF

3.1 MUSICAL HANDWRITING

The musical handwriting of composers has varied considerably. If you compare autograph manuscripts (holographs) in Figure 13, you can see how widely their musical handwriting ranges, from the untidy (Beethoven), via the stylish (Bach) to the meticulous (Stravinsky).

Nonetheless all these examples have to be legible, otherwise, of course, they would be useless. Neither players nor printers would take kindly to dealing with, for instance, orchestral parts of scores that were difficult to decipher. Yet, if legibility is one criterion of a good musical hand, so too, for the writer at least, is speed of execution. As we start to write notes on paper you will come to realize that most music takes much more time to notate than to play.

Therefore to minimize the time spent on what can become a miserable chore, one needs to cultivate a quick hand, and as with so much in this course, that means practice! In this section (and Section 6), you will be asked to write examples only once. But if you have the time, write them out several times, bearing in mind while doing so the two basic requirements: legibility and speed. In time you will then develop a neat, serviceable and even stylish musical hand.

We shall begin with Example 1, and since you will probably want to make alterations to your first attempts, write with a soft-leaded pencil and have an eraser to hand. We'll start with the treble clef. Unfortunately this is probably the most difficult clef to draw. We shall therefore take a little time to become familiar with its shape. Turn now to Video Section 1, 'Writing a treble clef'.

3.2 WRITING A TREBLE CLEF

 **VIDEO NOTES
UNIT 3, VIDEO SECTION 1**

Introduction

This video section takes you through the drawing of a treble clef. If you can already do this confidently, proceed to the next section of text.

NOW WATCH THE VIDEO SECTION.

After watching the video section

Practise drawing the treble clef in Example 14. First fill in the line of dotted clefs, and then draw clefs on the two blank staves where you are left to your own devices! Don't forget that the clef begins on the second line up from the bottom, and that the final downward line should lie more or less vertically but should not obscure that all-important starting point on the G line.

Example 14

3.3 WRITING NOTES USING THE TREBLE CLEF

Having practised writing a treble clef, return to your manuscript paper and insert a neat one there close to the left-hand end of the stave. The key signature (to be covered in Unit 6) usually comes next, but we do not need one here, so we can proceed on to the time signature. In Example 1 this is $\frac{4}{4}$.

Ensure that each number takes up only half of the stave, and that one is aligned under the other. (Note that there is no dividing line between the numbers, unlike a fraction.)

Now for the notes. As you will remember from Unit 1, Section 4.3, these should be drawn on the stave so that it is absolutely clear which pitch is intended. If the note-head is placed on a line, the line should run through the middle of the note-head. See Example 15.

Example 15

If the note is in a space, the note-head should not overlap a line.

Example 16

Otherwise, confusion might arise. For instance, at Example 16, note (a), is the pitch F or G? Since we are working in pencil, it takes a little time to fill in the note-heads, but the secret of writing out music quickly is to use a pen. Ideally it should have a nib thick enough to fill in the note-heads with as few strokes as possible, but not too thick for the staves and bar lines. You will be able to try this when you are less of a novice.

When drawing in the note-heads, ensure that they are evenly spaced. Since the horizontal axis represents time, it is better if notes of the same rhythmic value take up the same amount of space. Example 17 shows this. (For middle C, draw in the leger line first, then the head.)

Example 17

The note-heads are spread out more or less equally and the minims take up roughly twice the horizontal space of a crotchet. This looks better than:

Example 18

One final point about note-heads. They are somewhat more oval in shape than round. Indeed, the semibreve is clearly oval-shaped:

Example 19

We can now add the stems. The rule for stems when there is only one melody on a stave has already been mentioned (see Unit 1, Section 4.3). But as a reminder: a note on the middle line can have a stem going either up or down; a note below the middle line has a stem going up; and a note above the middle line has a stem going down.[2] Stems should be neither too long nor too short, and should be drawn vertically, not slanting to the left or right.

Example 20

Finally, we can draw a double bar at the end of the stave to mark the end of the piece and can add the tempo marking (now in Italian) in the relevant place. (We can omit the fingering since we know it from memory now.)

Example 21

Andante

Incidentally, notice that in the final three-note chord, the three note-heads are aligned vertically and the stem joins the three notes.

Before we proceed to write out our next example, bear in mind that one doesn't usually work in two stages as has been suggested here. You don't write in all the note-heads, and then add the stems. Each note is completed, both its head and stem, before you move on to the next. Occasionally, however, particularly when reducing an orchestral score, it is useful to be able to assess how the note-heads need to be arranged on the stave before adding the stems. But more about this in Unit 15, where two-stave reduction of scores is dealt with specifically.

---

[2]   For notes on the middle line, music publishers use various rules of thumb to decide the stem direction. For example, one 'rule' is that the direction should match that of most other notes in the same group or part of the bar. Tidiness is the final arbiter.

3.4 FURTHER EXAMPLES TO WRITE OUT

The second example we are going to write out consists of a variant of Example 11. It is given as Example 22.

Example 22

It has been varied so that rests and additional beams could be included. Beams (see Unit 1, Section 4.3) are used simply to group together the notes that require tails. The basic guideline is that at any point where the eye might become confused, the beaming should show clearly the main beats in the bar. Thus in bar 2, the division of the first beat into a quaver and two semiquavers is shown by beaming all three notes together as a group that adds up to a crotchet beat. Similarly for the last beat of bar 3. In the latter case, however, the preceding quaver is not joined on to the group because it forms a part of the second beat.

The rests included are the quaver rest ⅞ and the crotchet rest ⁊ (see Unit 1) and the latter, because of its unusual shape, needs a little practice before it is mastered. Try a few examples on a scrap of manuscript paper, making sure that the rest extends from just above the second line down the stave to just below the fourth line down, and that it is drawn vertically.

Example 23

Now write out Example 22. As with Example 21, ensure that notes with the same rhythmic value take up the same amount of space.

WRITE.

Now try playing your written-out version on your keyboard. Tap out the rhythm first, remembering that two quavers take up a crotchet beat, as do four semiquavers. The rhythmic pattern, quaver followed by two semiquavers (see bar 2), also takes up a crotchet beat as you can see from the beaming.

 TAP OUT THE RHYTHM, THEN PLAY.

Listen to the correct version on audio-cassette Item 6 if you need to check what you played.

 LISTEN NOW TO ITEM 6.

For our third and final example to write out, here is a variant of Example 12.

Example 24

This variant shows a straightforward use of beams in ⁶⁄₈, with the quavers grouped in threes to show the division of each bar into two main dotted-crotchet beats. There are some new signs too. The dot below a note indicates that you should play that note **staccato**, literally 'detached', releasing the note as soon as it sounds. The curved line encompassing groups of notes indicates the opposite, that the notes should be played **legato**, smoothly. These are the two most common signs for indicating how music should be articulated, and although you will not need to apply them to your harmony exercises, you will certainly need to be able to recognize them when score-reading. Listen to what this example sounds like (audio-cassette Item 7).

LISTEN NOW TO ITEM 7.

The curved line used in Example 24 is called a **slur**, and in vocal music indicates that a group of notes should be sung in one breath. Such curved lines are also used to indicate the phrase structure of a melody, and if you turn to Unit 4, you'll be able to see some examples of this (for instance, Examples 13–15).

Now write out Example 24 of this unit.

WRITE.

The three examples that you have just written out were restricted to the five notes middle C, D, E, F and G simply because these notes fit easily under the fingers when the thumb plays middle C. But keeping the hand in this position is too restricting; we need to move the hand to other positions so that we can play other notes. You will learn how to do this in the video extract 'Passing the thumb' so please turn to that now.

4 PASSING THE THUMB

 VIDEO NOTES
UNIT 3, VIDEO SECTION 2

Introduction

This video section is concerned with passing the thumb, which is a way of shifting the hand on the keyboard. In this way, a different set of notes is brought under the fingers. You will need your keyboard during the video section.

Before watching the video section

Video Example 1 shows the five-finger exercise that you should by now be familiar with.

Video Example 1

 NOW WATCH THE VIDEO SECTION.
YOU WILL ALSO NEED YOUR KEYBOARD.

During the video section

You are asked to play Video Example 2, with the fingering shown. When you are first asked to stop the tape you should concentrate on moving the thumb up a note in Video Example 2.

When you are next asked to stop the tape, you should concentrate on playing it in strict rhythm.

Video Example 2

As a result of playing Video Example 2 you can play three new notes, A, B and the C an octave higher than middle C. Video Example 3 gives the whereabouts of these new notes on the stave.

Video Example 3

The third time you are asked to stop the tape, you should play a mirror-image version of Video Example 2 with the left hand. Follow the fingering given, but move the thumb *down* a note where previously you moved it up a note. Once again practise this in two stages:

1   To get used to moving the thumb.

2   To get used to playing it in strict rhythm.

The next exercise is to play the notes in Video Example 4 with just one change of hand position.

Video Example 4

Video Example 5 shows where the position change happens.

Video Example 5

Video Example 6 shows the fingering to use. The thumb is passed under two fingers. Play it when you are asked to stop the tape the fourth time.

Video Example 6

Next you are shown how to pass the thumb under three fingers in order to play Video Example 7.

The fifth time you are asked to stop the tape, play Video Example 7. Practise it in two stages:

1   To get used to passing the thumb under three fingers.

2   To get used to playing it in strict rhythm.

Video Example 7

Video Example 8 gives the note names of the notes you played in Video Example 7

Video Example 8

Summary

I hope you were able to change hand positions successfully while working through the video extract. Considerable practice is needed to perfect the smooth movement of the thumb when changing hand position, but at least you are on the right track to perfection! Changing hand positions means that you can play additional notes, and at the end of the video section you played the scale of C major covering two octaves with your right hand. By changing hand position several times, yet more new notes can be played.

Notice the use of leger lines for notes above and below the stave:

Video Example 9

5 ACCIDENTALS

5.1 SHARPS

By this stage, you should be quite used to finding middle C and resting your fingers on the keyboard in readiness to play exercises starting on that note. In fact, the majority of the exercises you have played have started in that way. This time, however, let us move our hand position up one note and begin on D, covering the next four white notes, E, F, G and A, with your other fingers. We are going to play the following:

Example 25

Think about the rhythm first. This should present little difficulty since the notes are mostly crotchets, with only two minims occurring in bars 3 and 4. In addition, there is a very clear pattern, both as regards the rhythm and pitches. Bar 1 is repeated as bar 2, and bar 3 as bar 4. If we add the obvious fingering, we ought to be able to play these four bars more or less accurately at sight:

Example 26

 PLAY EXAMPLE 26.

Item 8 on the audio-cassette provides the correct version if you want to check what you played.

 LISTEN NOW TO ITEM 8.

Playing at the tempo marking *andante*, you may not have spotted that this is a well-known tune – or at least it's close to a well-known tune, but isn't exactly right. Try playing Example 26 quicker until you are playing it at a medium tempo (*moderato*). Do you recognize the tune now? If so, what is wrong with the notes as they appear at present? Which of them need changing? Try finding the right notes by playing various alternatives on your keyboard.

The tune consists of the opening bars of *Frère Jacques*, and it is the Fs that are wrong. To confirm this, play the tune again, but instead of playing F each time, move the middle finger up onto the black note that lies between F and G (see Figure 14).

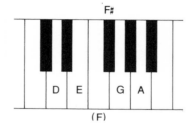

Figure 14

Repeat the tune slowly at first becoming familiar with the different position of the middle finger; then increase the speed.

Example 27

 PLAY EXAMPLE 27.

The new note we have played is called *F sharp*, and in order to notate this, a sharp sign (♯) is inserted before the relevant notes.

Example 28

This accidental, the sharp, can be inserted before any of the pitches, and always raises the pitch by the same degree. We have just noticed on the keyboard that the inclusion of a sharp alters the note F to the black note that lies immediately to the right of it, i.e. F♯. Similarly, G♯ is the black note that lies to the right of G, and A♯ is the black note that lies to the right of A (see Figure 15).

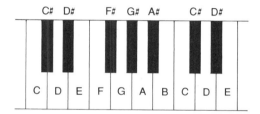

Figure 15

In each case the interval between the black note and its adjacent white notes is a **semitone**, the smallest interval to be found on your keyboard, and you will hear more about semitones when the construction of scales is discussed in Unit 6. However, for the present, notice that a semitone above E and B is not a black note but a white one, the notes F and C respectively. Therefore if we place a sharp before E and B, we find the E♯ on your keyboard is the same note as F, and B♯ the same note as C.

Example 29

E♯ = F   B♯ = C

E♯ and F might be notated differently, but they sound the same on the keyboard. Similarly with B♯ and C.

Before we move on to considering the other accidentals, flats and naturals, play audio-cassette Item 9. You will hear the opening of the slow, third movement of Mahler's First Symphony (1888), and the tune you hear (Example 30) bears a very close resemblance to Example 25.

Example 30

 LISTEN NOW TO ITEM 9.

All Mahler has done is add two notes (which do not make much difference) and, more importantly, change the F♯s of *Frère Jacques* to Fs. Mahler's music was inspired by a satirical picture of a huntsman mourned at his funeral by the birds and beasts he had pursued, and therefore the bright sturdiness of the original tune was unsuitable. By changing the F♯s to Fs, Mahler transformed the tune into something quite different.

Figure 16 Gustav Mahler (1860–1911). Austrian composer and conductor.

67

5.2 FLATS

We have seen that the sharp sign (♯) *raises* a note by a semitone. The flat sign (♭) *lowers* a note by a semitone. Play the following on your keyboard. It is the opening of *Frère Jacques* again, but beginning on F this time.

Example 31

Once again, are there notes that sound wrong for *Frère Jacques*? Which are they? By trying out various alternatives on your keyboard, attempt to find the right ones.

 PLAY.

The two Bs are incorrect and need changing into B♭s. B♭ is the black note that lies immediately to the left of B, shown in Figure 17.

Example 32

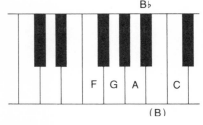

Figure 17

Play this through slowly at first, becoming familiar with the new position of the fourth finger, and then more quickly if you can.

 PLAY.

As with a sharp, a flat can be placed before any note and always lowers that note a semitone. Thus A♭ is the black note that lies immediately to the left of A, and so on (Figure 18).

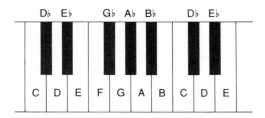

Figure 18

Where there is no black note available, as with F and C, the adjacent white note is used instead. Thus, on your keyboard, F♭ is the same note as E, and C♭ the same note as B.

Example 33

So we now have four white notes with two names each: E/F♭, E♯/F, B/C♭ and B♯/C. And we also have two names for each of the black notes. C♯ is the same note as D♭, D♯ is the same note as E♭, and so on. Which way you spell the notes depends on which scale you are using, a fact that will become apparent later during the course.

5.3 NATURALS

One more accidental occurs frequently, and that is the natural sign (♮). This is used to cancel a sharp or flat used previously in the bar. For example,

Example 34

Here the F♯ on the second beat changes to an ordinary F on the fourth beat. However, there are two rules to learn here. A bar line also cancels the accidentals used in a bar, so each bar is a fresh start, so to speak. In addition, if there are several successive Fs in a bar that we want to turn into F♯s, only the first needs a sharp sign. Try playing the following example bearing these rules in mind. The music looks daunting, but you will find the right notes with a bit of patience. The letters (a) to (e) over the music relate to my notes following the music.

Example 35

 PLAY EXAMPLE 35.

(a) The F has a sharp sign before it making it F♯.

(b) The F♯ at (a) is cancelled by the natural sign.

(c) A sharp sign is needed here because the F♯ in bar 2 has been cancelled by the bar line.

(d) This note is F♯ since the previous F in the bar has a sharp sign in front of it.

(e) The F♯ at (d) is cancelled by the natural sign.

Check that you had the correct version by listening to the recording in audiocassette Item 10.

 LISTEN NOW TO ITEM 10.

Finally, there are two other accidentals that you will probably come across during the course, although you may not have to write them. These are the double sharp (x), which *raises* the note *two semitones*, and the double flat (♭♭), which *lowers* the note *two semitones*. These occur for grammatical reasons too complex to go into here, but you need to be aware of them.

CHECKPOINT

> **Accidentals** are the signs used in staff notation to alter the pitch of a note by one or two semitones. A **sharp** raises the pitch a semitone; a **flat** lowers the pitch a semitone. A **natural** cancels a previous sharp or flat. Double sharps and double flats raise or lower a note respectively by two semitones.

6   NOTES ON PAPER II: THE BASS CLEF

So far, while putting our first notes on paper, we have concentrated on using the treble clef. But now we need to begin to familiarize ourselves with another clef since this is used for notating lower-register sounds. This clef is the bass or F clef, the latter name deriving from the fact that this clef signifies the whereabouts of the note F below middle C. (It was mentioned in Section 2.4.) As with the treble clef, you should practise drawing the bass clef several times, so please turn to the video section 'Writing a bass clef' now.

6.1   WRITING A BASS CLEF

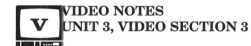 VIDEO NOTES
UNIT 3, VIDEO SECTION 3

Introduction

This video section takes you through the drawing of a bass clef. If you can already do this confidently, proceed to the next section of text.

NOW WATCH THE VIDEO SECTION.

After watching the video section

For further practice at writing the bass clef, first fill in the line of dotted clefs and then draw a succession of clefs free-hand on the lower two staves. In order to complete each clef, don't forget to add the two dots, one each side of the F line.

Example 36

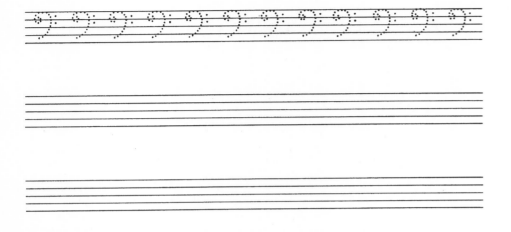

6.2 WRITING NOTES USING THE BASS CLEF

Having practised writing the bass clef several times, you can now write out your first example using this clef. The example is the five-finger exercise for the left hand (omitting the chord) you practised in Unit 2 Video Section 2. Remember that you started on middle C, moving throughout the exercise in the opposite direction to the right-hand version. Notice that whereas in the treble clef middle C was notated on the first leger line *beneath* the stave, in the bass clef middle C comes on the first leger line *above* the stave:

Example 37

Exercise 1

Write out the five-finger exercise for the left hand now. The answer can be found at the back of the unit (p. 73).

Discussion

You might have included a different tempo marking, although I expect you will now be able to manage to play the exercise at the tempo I suggested. You might also have included more repetitions of the down-and-up scalic pattern, and an easy way of doing this is to use a double bar line with **repeat marks** (dots). These are inserted at the start and end of the bars you want repeated, although it is assumed that the beginning of the piece marks the start of the repeat when the first double bar plus repeat marks is omitted. So in Example 38, with or without the opening double bar and repeat marks, bars 1–4 would be repeated.

Example 38

The notes you have written are the notes from C to F:

Example 39

C B A G F

By adding another three notes below the F we complete the scale of C major, which you have played already with the right hand during the video section on 'Passing the thumb':

Example 40

Now play this scale on your keyboard with your left hand using the rhythm and fingering as in Example 41. Remember to move your thumb along as you place your index and middle fingers on the notes B and A respectively in preparation for changing your hand position.

🎹 PLAY EXAMPLE 41.

Example 41

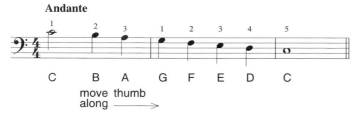

Repeat this scale as many times as it takes for you to be able to change hand positions comfortably. Then continue to play the scale, but now make a mental note of the names of the notes you are playing. Do this several times. In future units, you will need to be able to spot immediately which pitches these are and whereabouts they occur on your keyboard. Therefore a serious attempt to learn these note-names at this stage will pay considerable dividends subsequently. Do not proceed until you feel you are conversant with them.

Incidentally, now that you have learned both the treble and bass clefs, you can see how they relate to each other.

Example 42

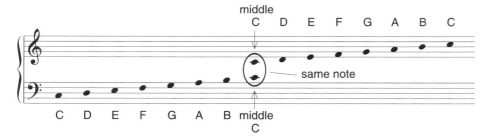

6.3 TRANSPOSITION

To conclude this section, and indeed the unit, here is some further practice at using the bass clef. We are going to *transpose* two of the music examples that appeared earlier in this unit so that they fit conveniently on the stave using the bass clef. Although the concept of transposition has not yet been explained, you have already experienced it. During the previous section, *Frère Jacques* was written out starting on both D and F. One version was, in fact, a transposition of the other; compare Examples 28

and 32. We shall begin by transposing Example 11 down an octave, using the bass clef (and a new tempo marking, *moderato*). Here is the original example:

Example 43

The first note is middle C and therefore the first note of the transposed version is the C an octave lower.

Exercise 2

Simply following the pattern of notes in Example 43, write out Example 43 transposed down one octave. If you need to check that you have not strayed from the correct pattern, check every so often that the note you are writing is an octave lower than the corresponding one in Example 43. Add letter names to the notes in your transposition if this helps you to focus your attention. The answer can be found at the back of the unit (p. 73).

Discussion

I hope you did not forget to include either the tempo marking or the time signature, since these both convey essential information. You will probably have had to take particular care that your note-stems were the correct way up (the stem on the D in the first bar could have gone either up or down), and that your note-heads sat neatly on the lines and between the spaces. Remember that the spacing out of the notes along the stave is also important. Play this example now to remind yourself of what it sounded like. (Start with the small finger of the left hand.)

PLAY EXAMPLE 46 (IN THE ANSWER TO EXERCISE 2, P. 73).

Exercise 3

Take the answer to the last exercise (Example 46) and write it out beginning on D. Check your version by playing it on your keyboard. Does your version sound right? If not, add an accidental to the note(s) that sound wrong. The answer can be found at the back of the unit.

Discussion

As with Example 28, you had to insert sharps before all the Fs to make the tune sound like the version starting on C.

Exercise 4

Transpose Example 44 so that it begins on the F lower than middle C. (Example 44 is the same as Example 24, but with a new tempo marking.) Check your new version by playing it, and remember to retain all the information given in the example in your new version. Again, you will have to add accidentals. The answer is on p. 73, opposite.

The answer is on p. 73, opposite.

Example 44

Moderato

CHECKPOINT

> **Transposition** takes place when music is written out at a different pitch from that in which it was originally conceived. Each note is raised or lowered by the same interval.

7 SUMMARY

As you worked through this unit, you will have spent most of the time either writing out music examples in staff notation or playing them on your keyboard. In other words, this has been primarily a practical unit. And this is because no matter how much theoretical knowledge you might gain about staff notation, it is through using it that you will become familiar with it. At first you will have found that dealing with staff notation has been a slow, frustrating process, but as you progress through the course, frequent practice will improve matters, and in time both writing staff notation and playing from it will become like second nature. Meanwhile, pause for a few moments to consider how far you have mastered the various skills listed below before proceeding to Unit 4. A little time spent reviewing your progress so far and taking remedial action where necessary will improve your chances of being able to tackle the new demands made on you in the next unit. Check, therefore, whether you can do the following.

1 Write out with reasonable accuracy and neatness the examples of staff notation using both the treble and bass clefs contained in the unit (Sections 3 and 6).

2 Play these examples on your keyboard. Some of them will necessitate changing your hand position and passing the thumb under smoothly (Video Section 2).

3 Remember and understand the Italian tempo and dynamic markings mentioned in Sections 2.6 and 2.7.

4 Identify easily the letter-names of notes written in the treble and bass clefs between the C below middle C and the C two octaves above middle C (Video Section 2 and Section 6.2).

5 Name fluently the notes on your keyboard lying between the C below middle C and the C two octaves above middle C (Video Section 2 and Section 6.2).

In addition, you should:

6 Be aware of the role of flats, sharps and naturals (Section 5),

ANSWERS TO EXERCISES

Exercise 1

Example 45

Exercise 2

Example 46

Exercise 3

Example 47

Exercise 4

Example 48

ACKNOWLEDGEMENTS

Figures 1, 4 and 6   Bibliothèque Nationale, Paris.

Figure 2   Bibliothèque Municipale, Valenciennes. Photo: La Boite à Images, Marly.

Figures 3 and 12(a)   British Library Board.

Figure 5   Private collection, courtesy of H.P. Kraus Rare Books (New York).

Figures 7, 8 and 11   Boosey and Hawkes Ltd.

Figures 13(a) and 13(b)   Staatsbibliothek zu Berlin, Preussischer Kulturbesitz, Musikabteilung.

Figure 13(c)   Paul Sacher Foundation, reproduced by kind permission of Boosey and Hawkes Music Publishers Ltd.

Figure 16   Mansell Collection.

Example 13   Schott and Company Ltd.

REFERENCE MATERIAL

NOTE VALUES (DURATIONS)

Name (American name in brackets)	Note	Rest	Relative length (division of semibreve)
breve (double whole note)			
semibreve (whole note)			
minim (half note)			
crotchet (quarter note)			
quaver (eighth note)			
semiquaver (sixteenth note)			
demisemiquaver (thirty-second note)			

Note the following alternatives: ⫿ is sometimes used for a breve; ꞊ is sometimes used for a crotchet rest.

TIME SIGNATURES

SIMPLE TIME

(basic pulse ♪, ♩, or 𝅗𝅥)

	quaver pulse	crotchet pulse	minim pulse
two beats per bar	2/8	2/4	2/2 (or ₵)
three beats per bar	3/8	3/4	3/2
four beats per bar	4/8	4/4 (or C)	4/2

COMPOUND TIME

(basic pulse ♩. or 𝅗𝅥.)

	dotted crotchet pulse	dotted minim pulse
two beats per bar	6/8	6/4
three beats per bar	9/8	9/4
four beats per bar	12/8	12/4

in simple time **triplets**

in compound time **duplets**

More complex beat divisions are shown on the same principle, e.g.

WHOLE BAR RESTS

The semibreve rest is used in every time signature, unless the total value of the bar exceeds a semibreve, when a breve rest is used.

CLEFS AND NOTE NAMES

Boxes show middle C.

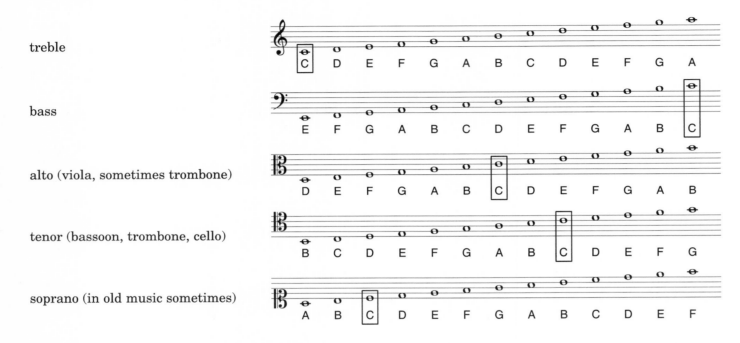

treble

bass

alto (viola, sometimes trombone)

tenor (bassoon, trombone, cello)

soprano (in old music sometimes)

Note. In modern scores, the tenor voice is often given in the treble clef, sounding an octave lower (often indicated by a small 8 below the clef).

ACCIDENTALS

♮ = natural

♯ = sharp, cancelled by ♮

♭ = flat, cancelled by ♮

𝄪 = double sharp

𝄫 = double flat

NOTE NAMES IN MAIN EUROPEAN LANGUAGES

The first three tables give all the chromatic inflections of the notes A, B and C. The principles can be extended to the remaining notes, D, E, F and G given in the fourth table.

	A♭♭	A♭	A♮	A♯	A𝄪
Eng.	A double flat	A flat	A (natural)	A sharp	A double sharp
Fr.	La double bémol	La bémol	La	La dièse	La double dièse
Ger.	Asas	As	A	Ais	Aisis
It.	La doppio bemolle	La bemolle	La	La diesis	La doppio diesis
Sp.	La doble bemol	La bemol	La	La sostenido	La doble sostenido

	C♭♭	C♭	C♮	C♯	C𝄪
Eng.	C double flat	C flat	C (natural)	C sharp	C double sharp
Fr.	Ut double bémol	Ut bémol	Ut	Ut dièse	Ut double dièse
Ger.	Ceses	Ces	C	Cis	Cisis
It.	Do doppio bemolle	Do bemolle	Do	Do diesis	Do doppio diesis
Sp.	Do doble bemol	Do bemol	Do	Do sostenido	Do doble sostenido

	B♭♭	B♭	B♮	B♯	B𝄪
Eng.	B double flat	B flat	B (natural)	B sharp	B double sharp
Fr.	Si double bémol	Si bémol	Si	Si dièse	Si double dièse
Ger.	Bes (Heses)	B	H	His	Hisis
It.	Si doppio bemolle	Si bemolle	Si	Si diesis	Si doppio diesis
Sp.	Si doble bemol	Si bemol	Si	Si sostenido	Si doble sostenido

	D	E	F	G
Eng.	D	E	F	G
Fr.	Re	Mi	Fa	Sol
Ger.	D	E	F	G
It.	Re	Mi	Fa	Sol
Sp.	Re	Mi	Fa	Sol

77

A214   UNDERSTANDING MUSIC:
ELEMENTS, TECHNIQUES AND STYLES

Unit 1   Introducing rhythm

Unit 2   More about rhythm; Introducing pitch

Unit 3   Starting with staff notation

Unit 4   Melody

Unit 5   Harmony I: The chord

Unit 6   Modes, scales and keys

Unit 7   Primary triads

Unit 8   Cadences

Unit 9   Following a score I

Unit 10   Formal principles I

Unit 11   First inversion chords

Unit 12   Secondary diatonic triads (II, III, VI and VII)

Unit 13   Modulation I

Unit 14   Following a score II

Unit 15   Two-stave reduction

Unit 16   Mostly revision

Unit 17   Harmonizing a melody I

Unit 18   Modulation II

Unit 19   Harmonizing a melody II

Unit 20   Following an orchestral score

Unit 21   Transpositions and reductions

Unit 22   Formal principles II

Unit 23   Baroque style study I

Unit 24   Classical style study I

Unit 25   Some points of style

Unit 26   Baroque style study II

Unit 27   Classical style study II

Unit 28   The Romantic period

Unit 29   Style, history and canon

Unit 30   Baroque style study III

Unit 31   Classical style study III

Unit 32   Towards the examination: Writing about music